INWARD JOURNEY

*Personal Psychological Stories & Perspectives
into Arab/Human Behavior*

DR. TALIB KAFAJI

authorHOUSE®

AuthorHouse™
1663 Liberty Drive
Bloomington, IN 47403
www.authorhouse.com
Phone: 1-800-839-8640

First published by AuthorHouse 3/1/2011

ISBN: 978-1-4520-8349-0 (sc)
ISBN: 978-1-4520-8350-6 (e)

Library of Congress Control Number: 2010914218

Printed in the United States of America

This book is printed on acid-free paper.

INTRODUCTION

I have been working as a psychologist for over 27 years. I have lived and worked in my beloved adopted country of America and I have now been working in the Middle East for last eight years. I have always wanted to share my professional and personal experiences with others. I thought, "It is time for me to get started and write the book that I have always dreamed of writing."

I had always suggested to my graduate students and supervisees when I taught them counseling and psychotherapy skills that the best model for treatment they could use with their patients was to bring their total being and their genuine self into the therapeutic process. Therefore, the advice that I gave my people I have to apply it in writing my book. I have to be wide open to the readers, with no pretence. In this book I am sharing the inward journey of myself and the people with whom I crossed paths as well as the ones who received professional help from me. Undoubtedly, the names of the patients have been changed for the sake of confidentiality. There are four sections in the book. It is comprised of 30 separate journeys, each one distinctively unique, perhaps in some of them the tone of sexuality is more pronounced. All the stories that I have cited in the book are real.

First: The personal inward journey through which I have gone was a series of metamorphoses and reassessments of my whole personality, from being an atheist wandering around the world and searching for the meaning of life in nearly 100 countries, to becoming a man with a profound faith and spirituality, from being a person who had a restless soul, to becoming a person who is anchored in the love of God, and from being an individual who suffered from bouts of depression, to becoming a person who is truly happy. For example, the Moroccan woman story was one of several mystical experiences that have shaped my life. The kindred spirit story is one which I have been unable to figure out and have no words to describe it. In my childhood I witnessed the honor killing, which is still in limited practice in some parts of the Middle East. Perhaps we need to accept certain events in life just as they are.

Second: The professional cases of treatment that I have presented here are those that I felt needed to be shared with readers as they can be of value to them. For example, the reincarnation case was mind-boggling to me and the Nadir and Aida story was a heart-wrenching one.

Third: My clinical observations about the Middle Eastern culture may appear to be critical at times. But, since I am a psychologist who has worked in both cultures and I was born in the Middle East, my observations are personal and seen through the eyes of an analytical psychologist. I feel compelled to share my perspectives. We in the Middle East must identify our shortcomings. We must not be like an ostrich who buries his head in the sand. While the Arab contributed greatly to the human community in terms of science and knowledge during the time of the Islamic renaissance, the present-day Arab, unfortunately, lags behind in contributions to the human community, except in a very limited area. Thus, the Arab must experience a self-awakening that addresses the following essential needs of the majority of the population: illiteracy, poverty, oppression, lack of justice, lack of freedom of expression, absence of creativity, and, most of all, regulate the unbridled greed or selfishness in their lives.

Fourth: The people with whom I met in my travels made contributions to my inward journey. For example, the Cuban doctor, the guru in India, and the friends in Abu Dhabi, as well as the women I dated or married had certain mystical qualities about them and of course some craziness as well.

This book is a collection of different thoughts, ideas, wisdom, experiences, encounters, and spirituality.

I intended to title the book, *Cocktail Thinking*, as it is a cocktail of thoughts. Over all, it is a humble gift to the readers to enjoy.

Talib kafaji
October 2009
Abu Dhabi

CONTENTS

1. The Story of My Underwear ... 1

2. Personal Strengths 7

3. Irrational Thinking 11

4. Is That Part of Human
   Nature? 17

5. Higher Self & Lower Self 21

6. Reincarnation 27

7. If You Want to be Happy for
   the Rest of Your Life Just Find
   Yourself a Moroccan Wife 33

8. Guilt Feeling 41

9. Psychology of Adam Story 49

10. The Triumph of Evil 57

11. Yearning for the Union 65

12. Wednesday Evening
    Discussion 71

13. The Meaning Of Our Life 79

14. The Psychology of the Desert
    Inhabitants 83

15. The Psychology Of Religions .. 87

16. Kindred Spirit 93

17. Ingredients for Happiness 99

18. Metaphysical Meaning of
    Illness 105

19. Honor Killing 111

20. Faithfulness 117

21. Everything Happens for a
    Reason 123

22. East is East . . . West is West,
    The Twain Shall Never Meet .. 127

23. The Cruelty of Family 133

24. Conversation with a Learned
    Man 141

25. Psychological Pollution 151

26. The Woman from Brazil 155

27. Psychological Incest 161

28. Box of Identity 171

29. The Prostitute of Hong
    Kong 175

30. Previous Life 183

The Story of My Underwear

On one winter morning in 1996, I entered a copy place well-known in Detroit, Michigan, called King's. I saw a regal, beautiful black woman who was radiating with sex and charm, and her legs were far better than Jennifer Lopez's legs. I went to her and said, "Good morning." She flashed her bright teeth and answered me back with such a pleasing manner. I collected my courage and asked for her- phone number. After that, we became close friends, and we dated for over two years.

In the second year she got pregnant from me, and we went to the abortion clinic to have an abortion. It was very hard on her, but not hard on me because of my fears of responsibility and insecurity about life. Then one day she came and asked me to marry her. Of course, as an insecure man and fearful of being committed to one person, I said, "No."

Pamela is a wonderful, highly educated woman. She is a worldly woman and very cultured, and most of all, she loves Tee, as she used to call me.

She left me and got married to a lawyer who turned out to be a dishonest person, and he cheated on her several times and did not respect her. The marriage lasted five years and, within those five years, she did not contact me, and I respected her marriage and hoped that she would find a life with this man.

Then the time came when I moved to work in Abu Dhabi in 2002. I found the love of my life with a Moroccan woman in Abu Dhabi, and I got married to Safa in 2004. She was a woman with such a rich soul.

She brought me back to a deep faith and love in God, which I had lost throughout the years that I spent wandering around the world. Although, the time that I was with Safa was a time of excruciating pain and agony, it resulted in a new spiritual birth of myself. Sadly enough, the marriage did not last long enough to work out our differences, and we got divorced in January, 2005. Still, the pain of losing a great partner was beyond any description, and I mourned the loss for a period of time, even though the old wisdom tells us that people come to our life either for a reason, or for a season, or for a lifetime. It seemed Safa came to my life for a reason, the spiritual revival of my soul.

Then, one day Pamela contacted my friend in Detroit and got my number in Abu Dhabi. She called me up and said that she had gotten divorced, and she would like to come to see me and explore the possibility of us being together again. Of course, I welcomed the idea, as I was very lonely after the divorce. She came in the winter of 2005, and we had great times with such fabulous spiritual sexual experiences, because every part of her body radiates with sexuality. I could not have enough of kissing every inch of her marvelous body.

One day I was changing my underwear before her, and she saw a mark around my waistline, and she asked, "Why do you have such a noticeable mark around your waistline?"

The answer was obvious--that was a result of wearing tight underwear for many years. She said, "Why in the world don't you wear wider underwear?"

I said to her, surprised, "Would they have a wider one?"

She said, "Of course!"

I said, "I really did not know, or I knew, but throughout the years I got used to the discomfort of wearing tight underwear and never paid attention to the mark around my waistline."

Pamela took me to the mall in Abu Dhabi and she purchased for me 6 pairs of wide comfortable underwear and said to me, "Wear them now, and you can feel the difference."

When I started to wear them, I felt so good and had no more discomfort of wearing tight underwear.

✤ ✤ ✤

The merit of this story shows the ultimate in human stupidity. We, as a people, are inclined to get used to the pain or discomfort in our lives if we do it long enough, and we do not think to change it. I have tolerated all those years wearing tight underwear without even thinking to change it.

That is exactly what is happening to us as human beings. We live under such pain and misery, but we do not like to change. Either we are unaware of the possibility of such change, or we think this is all we have in life. The feeling of being worthless often time tends to be buried in our unconscious mind. Thus, we periodically need to have a serious examination of our life, and see if we are experiencing anything that may bother us or cause some pain to us. Then we can try to change it or move away from it.

However, the sad fact of life is that deep down in the recess of our unconscious mind we believe that we do not deserve to be happy. Therefore, we stay or tolerate physical or psychological pain. Try not to go far and just look around and see how many people are in serious physical pain, and do not take any steps to correct it or try to heal themselves. If you ask them, "Do you want to be happy and healthy?" the answer is, "Of course, I want to be happy and healthy," but they do not want to do the hard work. As the old wisdom states, "Everyone wants to go to heaven, but no one wants to die". How in the world can you get to be in heaven unless you die first? If you want to be happy and healthy, then there is a part of you that must die so you can allow the healthy part to flourish.

There are few people in the world who understand that life is a journey of joy, on the contrary, others think life is a journey of pain and discomfort. We can see that clearly all over people's faces and attitudes. The best example is me who lived all those years with tight underwear and did not understand that there was some comfortable underwear on the market.

Maybe, we are oblivious to the things around us or to the pain that we have. It takes a person to be a psychologically minded individual to understand the complexity of their being. The biggest challenge to us as a human being is to know the good and the bad for us. We may think that we know, but reality shows us the opposite. However, if we do not treat ourselves well, then we cannot treat others well. The fundamental concern here is to identify the pain or the discomfort in one's life so we can change. We also need to learn the skills to change and to become healthy and happy human beings. Consequentially, the world around us will be a happy and healthy place. And as the old wisdom goes, "If I am happy, the world is happy, and if I am miserable, then I will make the world around me miserable as well". These attitudes or thoughts are contagious and thus, we really need to be very mindful about them.

This concept may lead us to a bigger concept which is the love for ourselves. If we have it, then we have it for others, but if we do not have it, then our heart is empty, and that can be a catastrophe.

There is a metaphoric story in which a group of angels were asked by some humans, "Tell us, what heaven is?" Their answer was, "We cannot describe heaven, but we can say the closest thing to heaven is the heart with love." Then, they were asked, "Tell us, what hell is?" Their answer was "the heart that has no love."

Human beings are born with a tendency to be unhappy because of the mishaps that happened to our ancestors throughout the years on the earth. They suffered a lot in their lives and that stays in our collective conscious. We need to do the serious work in life to undo the damages that have been inflicted on us, whether from our parents, or from our unconscious, or from the people around us. To be happy and free from any psychological or physical pain is our ultimate task. Again, by nature, we are lazy creatures, we do not like to work hard, but we just like to take it easy. Thus, we need to challenge our nature and try to work to be healthy and happy.

Throughout my limited years on the planet Earth and in working as a psychologist for many years in different cultures, I have observed that people, in general, do not know how to be happy. As our beloved father, Sigmund Freud, said "There is pleasure in pain and misery."

Being happy or healthy physically or psychologically requires a lot of work and skills. We need to draw a lesson from all these concepts and hold it dear to our heart. We need to learn it or be around people who point it out to us, and that is what my beloved friend Pamela did on her last trip to Abu Dhabi. If she had not pointed it out to me, I would be still wearing tight underwear and suffering silently.

So, please do not suffer silently, try to find your own Pamela to show you how to free yourself from the tight underwear. I am certain that most of us wear metaphoric tight underwear. We are living a mediocre life without examination or enjoyment.

Plato said, "An unexamined life is not worth living". Now you are faced with the challenge that there is immensity in living joyfully. Do not accept the mediocrity in your life-style. Be unique and compassionate in your life.

PERSONAL STRENGTHS

We all as, individuals, aspire to be strong in many areas in our life because we are born with certain limitations, and we may spend our life trying to overcome these limitations. There is no human being who is free from such limitations or shortcomings, either physically, mentally, emotionally, or spiritually. Some of us are aware of these limitations, while the rest of us are not. Of course, the ones who are unaware of such limitations are the fortunate ones, while the ones who are aware of them may suffer and may spend a good portion of their time making up for the undeveloped part of them. There is an old Chinese saying that says, "He who seeks knowledge seeks sorrow." In other words, ignorance is a blessing because if one does not know, then there is no need to try, but if one knows, the trouble may start. It depends upon the way you look at it.

We must know that when we are born, we are a half-developed being, and we need to strive to complete the unfinished business of our personal development. Thus, we have to have an awareness of the unfinished pieces in order to make the change in these areas. Perhaps we will go through life with a serious developmental problem and will not mind it at all. Hence, we will talk about the individual who wants to change in order to make their life more meaningful and enjoyable. The change can also make you more effective and invigorated and can enrich your personality for as long as you live. Perhaps people will say, "Why should I change?" The answer is clear. If you live comfortably with your self inside of your skin, then there is no need for a change. As they say, "Do not scratch where it does not itch." But, if you feel that there is some itching in one or two areas of your life, then you may benefit from the steps outlined below.

There are four areas in which you can build your personal strength: physical, emotional, mental, and spiritual. The road maps for improving each of them are as follows:

Physically

Undoubtedly, physical health is the springboard for a joyful life. Moreover, being physically healthy is a full-time job because the abundance of health does not come easily and you have to do something every day that makes your health better. The most important challenge that we face is our laziness because we, as individuals, are born with the inclination to be lazy. However, there are a few necessary steps that any individual can follow to obtain good health and vitality. Furthermore, you must assign a time to each step and never postpone what you may need to do to get the health that you desire. As they say in the old Native American wisdom, "Try to carry your body in the first 40 years correctly and then your body will carry you for the next 40 years of your life."

Strict adherence to the following principles will allow you to have abundance of health.

1. Every morning drink four glasses of water on an empty stomach which will clear up all the blockages in the body activate the digestive system and remove the sediments.
2. After drinking the water in the morning, eat fruits.
3. Try to restrict yourself to a single food family which means try to eat each food family separately and do not mix fruits with proteins, or carbohydrates with proteins. Just eat them separately. Focus mainly on eating vegetables.
4. Do not eat food that has a lot of sugar in it. Use natural sweeteners like honey or figs.
5. Eat small meals throughout the day, following the grazing principle.
6. Watch your circadian rhythm, which means your sleep cycle. Sleep during a certain time and wake up at a specific time.

7. Exercise daily, choosing an exercise that is suitable to you.

8. If you notice any complaints from your body, it can be a warning sign. Try to correct it immediately to bring your body into total balance.

Emotionally and Mentally

1. Train and tame your mind to think positive and have a bright interpretation of any circumstance. Hold the leash so the horse of your thoughts can be restrained.

2. Find yourself a supportive, encouraging partner. This is the backbone of emotional health. Do not fall into the pit of alienation or loneliness.

3. Be expressive and direct in what you think and what you need. In other words, be assertive.

4. Try to learn to play a musical instrument which can cultivate your sensitivity.

5. Sharpen your mind through intellectual challenges, through investigation of the truth and do not be a parrot.

6. Have some passion for what you do in your life.

7. Surround yourself with positive and uplifting people.

8. Free yourself from fears and anxiety.

9. Learn to meditate and relax.

10. Let go of anger for it can pollute your soul and be forgiving of yourself and others.

Spiritually

1. Develop a close relationship with the original source of your being, the eternal power of the universe [God].

2. Nurture yourself and others by giving and receiving unconditionally.

3. Accept the demonic side of you and find a happy marriage between the ugly and the beautiful side of yourself. We all have both sides.

4. Seek union with the universe and avoid judgment and separation from other fellow humans.

5. Be mindful that this life is transient. It is a rehearsal for the infinite one, so do not become attached to the green (money).

Conclusion

The principles pertaining to each of these areas were investigated thoroughly, both scientifically and at the individual experience level, and undoubtedly proved to be of great value for personal development. Thus, try to have a plan of action to implement these principles. Bear in mind that when you go to your job and work hard, you are doing that so you can make a living. Because if you stay home you might starve and this is like working to gain something. So when you work on your physical, mental, emotional, or spiritual health, you also gain something-- strength and sustenance in your personality--something every one of us desires. While illness or malfunctions can be the result of an imbalance in any one of these areas, the focus here is on how to actualize your personal strength and gain optimal health in all these areas.

Irrational Thinking

I f we look closely at our daily behavior, we will conclude that the majority of our behaviors can be irrational. The questions that arise might include the following. Why are we such irrational beings? Is this part of our genetic evolution, or psychological makeup, or collective consciousness, or just a cultural conditioning? Or, do all these factors, together, contribute to our irrationality? In this inward journey we will focus first on the phenomena of irrational thinking and, second, on what makes us irrational creatures.

First let us explore what constitutes irrational behavior. Bear in mind that thinking produces behavior. If we closely examine our behavior and motivation, we will be stunned to see that irrationality is deeply rooted in our personality, and it can be manifested in the following attitudes and traits of our behaviors.

A primary trait of irrationality is that of the self-destructive tendency. No single human being is free of this tendency. For example, we may engage in overeating, smoking, or using drugs. Even though we are very aware of the harmful effects of such engagement, we do it anyway. With complete disregard for our physical and mental health, we might also engage in activities that can bring serious harm to us or become involved in risky behavior that can bring us closer to death. We do these things without hesitation, and we may even derive some sort of thrill from such behaviors. Needless to say, our daily life is filled with many examples of these activities, from gambling to car racing to bungee jumping, just to name few.

A second component of irrationality is our adherence to the concept of nationality in that some of us wage war just to defend the land or the country in which we live. We are indoctrinated that protecting our country by going to war can be evidence of national pride or a sacred thing to do. We have shed a lot blood just for the sake of nationality, which can be viewed as the ultimate absurdity of human irrational thinking. Let us look at it from the point view of rational thinking. The accident of birth dictated the location of our birthplace, to be born in Brazil or China, so why in the world have we developed an adherence or an attachment to a place that we did not choose in the first place? If your mother met your father in Mali, then you will be Malian; or if your father married your mother in Mexico, then you are Mexican. So, where is the logic here? When we are born in a place merely by accident and then develop an attachment to that place to such a degree that we become neurotic about it clearly shows human foolishness.

A third observation about our irrational thinking is that we tend to think our ethnic group of people is better than another people. For example, the Arabs may feel they are better than others, and the Indians may feel they are better than the Chinese, and the Spanish may feel they are better than the Portuguese, and so on. This can be the seed for animosity or hatred. An individual may have a false sense of pride in belonging to a specific group of people. Again, the accident of birth dictated that you are part of that ethnic group of people, so why do you think your "brand" of people is better than the other "brand"? This thinking can be a prejudice thought which feeds into irrational behaviors. Such thinking has brought a lot of pain and suffering to the human community because of the superior attitudes we hold towards one another. For example, the tragic concept of slavery was based on such an attitude, that I am better than another.

A fourth observation of irrational behavior is the tendency to be greedy; undoubtedly, greed is most often associated with fear. For example, we want more and more, and the more we have, the more insecure we become in losing what we have. Thus, we keep hoarding. A case in point here is the fear of a rich individual that he may lose his wealth; thus, he keeps accumulating. It is very rare that we, as a people, stop and say, "Enough!" and simply enjoy what we have. On the contrary, we keep running in the vicious circle of greed because the trick of irrational thinking tends to paralyze us and take over our faculty of reasoning.

A fifth component of irrational thinking is that of our real or imagined fears and anxiety. We are anxious over some things that do not even exist. Our life is filled with anxiety, and the things that we are anxious over may never happen. Worry or anxiety is very disturbing to us, and it can take the joy out of our life, but we keep worrying anyway. Fears also play major roles in our life. The most common fear is the fear of what other people may think of us, the fear of being judged by others. Similarly, we fear the unknown; since it is unknown, why should we fear it? It is such a paradoxical way of thinking. This is why we suggest to people that psychological therapy can be of great value in freeing them of the burden of anxiety and fears.

The sixth component of irrational thinking is that, in most instances, we tend to seek misery, rather than happiness. We have all that it takes to be happy, but we just cannot believe it or act upon it. Our dysfunctional thinking prevents us from doing so, and it can be a stumbling block to joyful living because we have been told that life is a painful journey, even though our reality suggests otherwise.

The seventh component of irrational behavior is that we tend to live a chaotic life as far as our physical health is concerned. We ignore our health by not paying serious attention to symptoms that may appear, or we do not allocate time to the health and maintenance of our body, including exercise or selection of proper food. This is why we see the majority of people over the age of 50 taking two to three medications daily.

The eighth observation of irrational thinking is obsessive thinking. This can represent the peak of our irrationality. We keep the record of past events playing in our mind even though we are aware that it will not produce any results, bring anything of value to our life, or bring about any change. Yet, we keep playing it. Basically, we are slaves to the garbage of the past. We are mentally so tired of this rumination, but we are unable to stop it. The stream of our irrational thoughts can be very powerful once it has established a pathway in our brain.

The ninth observation of irrational behavior is that we may stay in very painful or meaningless situations because a negative frame of mind provides us with all sorts of justifications for keeping us away from the good life. While deep down we know it is stupid to stay in such situations, we are fettered by the situations. For example, we stay in a boring and lifeless relationship, or meaningless job. Or, sometimes we may clip our wings by our own hands and say, "I cannot fly." Undoubtedly, this is a very self-defeating behavior.

After the insightful journey through the ninth phenomena of our irrational thinking/behavior, we conclude that we are irrational beings. Nevertheless, we now need to examine the causes of our irrationality that have robbed the joy from our lives.

Evolutional psychology tells us that our ancestors suffered for a long time from the harsh lifestyle they lived. At that time, man was not able to subjugate or control the environment as he now does. He was at the mercy of the weather and the environment: the heat and the cold, earthquakes, shortages of food or water, and animal attacks. He was helpless in the face of it all. The life span was very short, and man did not reach the age of 40 because of diseases and illness. All of these collective hardships have been passed on from generation to generation and imprinted on our conscious mind, our archetypes, as Carl Jung calls them. Therefore, our irrationality and negative outlooks tend to dominate our behavior.

Another cause of our irrational behavior is that we are conditioned by a negative society or a negative upbringing. The irrationality tends to take over our being. A painful part, and the most crucial one, is that most of us come from parents who are not skilled in teaching us how to think rationally, and they do not give us the tools to dispute irrationality because the whole society functions irrationally. We never learn critical thinking. On the contrary, they taught us directly or indirectly that we have to follow the herd and not be active participants in our lives.

The final analysis of our irrational behaviors, according to Sigmund Freud, is that there is a constant struggle between the two parts of our personality--the death wish (thanatos) and the survival wish (eros)--and the death wish sometimes takes over the survival wish. Thus, we see that irrational behavior is a prevailing one in our daily lives. Therefore, we are inherently irrational beings, and we are the cause of our own suffering and pain.

In the above passages we identified the facets of our irrational behaviors and the causes of them. However, if we want to venture out and trim away some of those behaviors, we may need to develop a different level of awareness. As Albert Einstein said, "Problems cannot be solved at the same level of awareness that created them." Thus, it is imperative that we develop a new level of awareness in order to tackle our irrationality.

Nevertheless, one effective approach is to go deep down to the roots of our irrational behavior and try to unplug it. Needless to say, this is done with the help of psychology science. Although such fundamental changes in our thinking and behavior can be an overwhelming challenge, the value of such a project can be extremely worthwhile. And, it can be done on two levels—on the group level, through the educational system or any other institution, and on the individual level through the wonderful science of psychoanalysis, which can unveil the irrationality of our thinking, or through cognitive psychology, which may identify the sources of our disturbance. By then we may free ourselves from the dysfunctional thoughts, and live as a rational being.

Is That Part of Human Nature?

Working with people as a psychologist for over 25 years has given me in-depth perspectives regarding human nature. As a result of seeing people for psychotherapy, I have developed three perspectives about people's behavior and attitudes.

First Perspective

People are generally inclined to seek their misery, not their happiness. As we all know, the common belief is that people seek their happiness. This is not true, and it is a figment of our imagination. Look around you. You do not need to be a scientist in human behavior to see how many people are happy and joyful. Perhaps, you can count them on your fingers. The majority of us are miserable beings, whether we are rich or poor, educated or illiterate, or rulers or followers. It does not make any difference.

You may ask me the question, "Do you really mean it?" I will say "yes." And the second question you may ask is "Why?" Then I will say, "There are some reasons that drove me to come up with such conclusions." Here are several of them.

1. Our ancestors lived very harsh lives for millions and millions of years, and they encountered a lot of Nature's trouble--earthquakes, cold, harsh winters or the heat of the desert or the animals that ate them up or lack of food and wars between them over natural resources, diseases and many other hardships. These experiences are fixed in our conscious mind

and sometimes we inherit them from generation to generation. Thus, as a by-product of our experiences, we are gloomy, pessimistic, and illogical beings.

2. We are a very fragile people. Illness can very easily overcome us and leave us feeling helpless. We as human beings are aware of our fragile nature. For example, a tiny bacteria or virus can paralyze us in a second. And, that can feed upon our brittle nature. Needless to say, this is not a romantic view about us.

3. We live among uncultivated people, who are jealous and envious by nature, and when they see you happy or well, they tend to throw at you some of their personal disturbances. Hence, the majority of us tend to internalize such disturbance, and that can take away some of the joy from our life.

4. We as human beings tend to have self-pity, and it may give us a psychologically soothing effect. Then, the people around us pity us, as well. That feeling may give us a sense of weakness.

5. There is pleasure in pain. This concept can be attributed to the psychoanalytic theory that we, as individual tend to derive joy from pain. Perhaps, we call those people masochists; however, almost every one of us has some masochistic tendencies. This means that we inflict either psychological or physical pain on ourselves.

6. We, as individuals come into this world out of the pleasure of two people who, in most instances, either have no love for each other, or do not understand the meaning of having a child. Then, we, as individuals, become aware of complexities in the relationships between our parents and develop a dislike of ourselves. That can contribute to our own misery.

Second Perspective

People tend to seek illness and avoid health; to be physically healthy can be a very challenging and overwhelming job. It is required that an individual know the rules of basic health. Schools do not teach us how to be physically healthy, let alone how to be psychologically healthy. So, people have no knowledge in this area. Being healthy is a full-time job, and the majority of us are fabulously lazy. For example, how many people brush their teeth right after eating the meal? Not too many, because the bacteria tend to attack us as long as there is some food left in our mouth. This is just a simple fact of hygiene.

But what about eating the right food? Normally, we do not have knowledge on what to eat. Foods tend to be divided into several families. For example, the family of protein tends to dislike the family of carbohydrates; the family of fruits tends to disagree with the family of protein. But, we tend to mix all the food together, and then we have serious health problems. Thus, the majority put the wrong fuel into their body. For example, diabetes, high blood pressure, high cholesterol, and acid in the stomach are just a few of the diseases that result from the wrong fuel being put into the body.

Another part of being liked is to be sick, originated in the early years of our life. When we were children, we got a lot of attention if we got sick. Sometimes, we even faked it just to get our parents' love and attention. That feeling can stay with us into adulthood as we seek such attention for the wrong reasons. Nevertheless, there are extreme cases of hypochondria.

Overall, we do not adhere to the rules of basic health. For example, look around you and see the epidemic of obesity in the world. People try to kill themselves by their teeth. As they say, it is not *what* you eat, it is what *eats* you.

Third Perspective

We, as a people, tend to run away from freedom and seek enslavement. You may say that this is not true; we love freedom. Reality gives us a concrete example of our fascination with creating shackles for ourselves.

Our ancestors lived very free lives for millions of years, but modern man has created his own shackles. People used to roam around from land to land without any passport, or boundaries, or even police control. Look what we have done to ourselves; we confined ourselves to one small country and, if we want to travel, we have to have a proper document. That is just one example of losing our freedom.

We used to manage our life without the computer system. Our ancestors lived millions of years without computers, and they did well. Imagine, now, if the computer system stopped. Our lives would be basically paralyzed. That is not freedom; we are slaves to the machine. Perhaps, you say that computer usage is advancement. It can be, but at the expense of our freedom.

We also used to be free of any kind of commitment to marriage. Then, humans invented the institution of marriage. (Please, do not mistake me in this. I am just trying to illustrate examples of our previously free life.) Then, man and woman become slaves to each other.

Erich Fromm wrote a book called *Escape from Freedom* in which he clearly showed that human beings have imprisoned themselves in small boxes and have given it a different and fancy name; they call it "nationality." They may call it "love of land" which is the ultimate in stupidity.

Another part of our enslavement is the psychological shackles that our mind has manufactured for us [Anxiety]. This can be detrimental to our inner peace and creativity. For example, we consider that our present time is a time of anxiety. Our mind has forged a maniacal state. Anxiety has imprisoned us and paralyzed us. Fears have dominated our thinking and our attitudes, whether these fears are real or imagined. Guess what? Ninety percent of our fears are imagined. Thus, we are not free, internally or externally.

With freedom, there is a responsibility, and we often run away from such responsibility. We assign our responsibility to others and let them lead us. Of course, that is an absurd and foolish act.

In the Middle East part of the world there is another kind of shackle, the cult of personality. People are overvalued, or admired, or even worship the people who have power & money. Great numbers of people are followers and are not free individuals. Perhaps they may possess the herds' mentality. It is safer to follow and less challenging. Freedom also requires emotional maturity. The sad fact is that majority of people particularly in Middle East are not mature enough to conduct or manage themselves responsibly. As a result of our collective attitudes, we, as people in general, are less free.

Higher Self & Lower Self

Human individuals are not born a blank slate as many behavior scientists profess. We are born with a certain potential for being benevolent or mischievous; good or evil, [we have both sides; Mother Teresa & Saddam]. And, that may depend upon two factors--the environment into which we were born, like our parental upbringing as well as the genetic predisposition. If the environment is healthy and our parents are aware of their crucial roles, then our contributions to ourselves as well as to our fellow humans can be uplifting and promoting. If the environment is impoverished in many aspects and our parents are ignorant, then we grow up with serious psychological limitations. As far as genetic inclination concerns, perhaps the intervention here is limited one.

We can be more specific about the meaning of those two aspects of our personality. The good, or the benevolent, part we might call "the higher self," and the mischievous part we might call "the lower self." Moreover, these concepts were clearly stated in all the books of religions. Thus, there is always a struggle inside every individual between the higher self and the lower self.

The higher self can be defined as the disposition or the inclination to the sense of justice, forgiveness, freedom, caring about others, compassion, helpfulness, being giving, and respect for fellow humans. On the other hand, the lower self is the disposition or the tendency of being envious, jealous, aggressive, selfish, violent, greedy, lazy, and oppressive of others.

This question may present itself: How do we communicate with sides of the self, the higher and the lower? We may say that it depends upon society, and our parents. For example, if society promotes individual freedom, a sense of justice, kindness, and a respect for law, then we may cultivate this corner of the higher self. And if our parents attend to our emotional needs and value us as a human being then we can grow as a healthy individual. But if society lacks freedom and a sense of justice and parents abuse us, then maybe we can tap into the rubbish of the lower self. Hence, the focus of this journey on societal and environment contributions. Because being good parents tend to depend on individual family in either culture.

Let us examine the application of these two concepts in reality. In the western world, individual freedom exists, the rules of the law are respected and individual rights and privileges are guaranteed. In such cases, the tendency is towards cultivation of the higher self. Consequently, there is a place for creative activities, and members of the society can thrive and flourish. On the contrary, in the Arab world, lack of freedom and a sense of justice may bring the characteristics of the lower self out in full swing, showing in jealousy, envy, aggression, lack of respect for human values, and a lack of creativity.

There is one caveat that needs to be made. The presentation is not an absolute sense regarding western or eastern societal characteristics; it is just in relative terms. No doubt, the western society has its own deficits, and it can tap into the lower self at times. And, the Arab society may tap into the higher self at times. But, the overall observations are that the western society has evolved to address the needs of the higher self, while the Arab society is still not ambitious enough to tackle those needs.

Fundamentally speaking, if a society lacks freedom, which is considered the antidote for the human soul, individuals will show the repulsive side of their personality. The lack of freedom and the oppression in the Arab world has brought the worst out of the people. This is why we see the dark side of the Arab individual prevailing these days.

Constitutionally, Arabs are not a bad people, but oppression throughout their long history has marginalized their personalities and has twisted their perceptions. Thus, they became the source of disturbance to themselves as well as to others.

The kernel of truth is that each individual inherently carries the seed of corruption as well as the seed of goodness in his /her personality makeup. Which seed grows depends upon the ground on which the seed falls. Because of the oppression and lack of freedom, the Middle Eastern society has fertile ground in which the seed of corruption can germinate and has been the norm of their lives. It has stripped the Arab individual of his humanity and left him empty with eyes wide open for revenge and aggression. This is why freedom can be the ultimate goal for psychological health and is the panacea for human growth. Freedom is the healer for a lot of societal illness. Freedom and a sense of justice can bring out the beauty of an individual. This is why we see a lot of intellectual development in the West and its absence in the East. The oppression, the unfair treatment, and the lack of freedom in the Arab world causes the Arab individual to be in a constant of fighting with his family, in the work place, on the street, and within him/herself simply because his needs, desires, and wishes have not been fulfilled.

Freedom and a sense of justice and equality are not luxuries; they are necessities and indispensable parts of an individual's psychological wellbeing. Western thinkers have recognized that fact for a long time, and they have established and built up a society that nurtures such functions. Our thinkers, as well, have realized that and sacrificed their lives, but to no avail. Somehow, the oppression became a fabric of Middle Eastern society. The challenge for all of us is to weed it out, even though it can be a very colossal task. However, most of the people in the Middle Eastern society are tired of looking for pieces of bread for their families in spite of the enormous amount of wealth in this part of the world.

As a result of the long history of oppression and lack of freedom in the Arab world, a painful fact presents itself--the Arab psychology became very allergic to freedom and a sense of justice. Even the educated people reject it and say, "Freedom does not fit our society. We are a people always needing to be controlled by the rollers." It's as if the people in this part of the world are wild animals and need to be caged. When people live for such a long time under oppression and the lack of freedom, their minds become fossilized, and they reject anything that may bring them a challenge for growth or development. Because the channel of communication has been directed towards the lower self for a long time, there has been complete negligence of the higher self.

Anyone who works in behavior science understands that there are no bad people or good people. People can have both inclinations, but society may orient its members one way or the other and promote or demote their values. The Arab has been subjected to such treatment for so long that oftentimes they do not even question their status quo. They got used to it, and they do not know, or have ever experienced anything different. Although, a large numbers of them have visited the West, have seen the life there, perhaps, may wish to live that kind of life, they would not do anything to change their own life. Instead, they merely accept their meaningless existence. The Arab individual has lost his sense of courage; he/she has become psychologically weak and ingratiated their way to the people in power. Painfully, they accepted for themselves to be only voracious consumers of Western materialisms and have not accepted the core values of the West.

The Arab society has been infected by a sense of helplessness because the characteristics of the lower self have been in full operation for such a long time, while the higher self has been dwarfed. In some societies we may sometimes observe struggles between the higher self and the lower self. However, in Middle Eastern society, such struggles are very rare. In fact, we may see the complete submission and acceptance of an individual's humiliation.

Conclusions

Each person inherently carries healthy values and pathological values. We may call these the higher self and lower self, or the dark side of the self and the bright side of the self. Our beloved father, Sigmund Freud, called them the superego and the Id. If the surrounding society and parents are healthy, the communication can be directed toward the higher self. That can bring out the best in a person. If the surroundings are unhealthy, the communication tends to take place with the lower self, and that can bring out the worst in a person.

The over-arching wisdom is that a society should structure itself in such a way as to tap into the core of the individual higher self, rather than flirts with the dark side of the soul. At the present time, the Arab society may need a serious self- reflection or self-examination to eradicate the tyranny of the culture and establish a free society. Once a society does that, the higher self will thrive, and the resulting contributions can be immense to the individual as well as to the rest of the people.

REINCARNATION

I was in Detroit, Michigan in 1998 and was working as a clinical psychologist in one of the community mental health system programs. Normally, these clinics tend to deal with all sorts of populations. Marvin, a Vietnam veteran [this is not real name], was referred from the veteran's hospital for the treatment of mental illness with the diagnosis of schizophrenia.

Personal History

Marvin was 48 years old, divorced, with one son and one daughter. He was a veteran of the Vietnam War. Marvin grew up on the east side of Detroit. He went to high school and after he graduated from high school, was recruited by the United States Marines. He served for over four years in the army. It seemed that he had developed a mental illness while he was in his last year of duty. After his discharge, he started to seek treatment at the veteran's hospital, but he did not like it and went to several clinics. He was then referred to me for long-term psychotherapy.

Normally, in the clinic we take a very detailed history of the patient's life. Marvin was an average student in high school, he was not involved in any trouble, and he was a rather private person. There was no sign of any mental trouble. He had one brother older than himself, and both parents were deceased. They came from a working class family. His father had worked for the Ford Motor Company and was retired from there. His mother was a housewife with a limited education.

Employment History:

When Marvin joined the army he went through thorough physical and mental examinations. His records indicated there was no sign of any mental illness. Marvin witnessed the atrocities of the war. He saw his friends killed in front of him, and he was unable to help them out. He was taken by the North Vietnam soldiers and imprisoned for two months before being freed by his fellow comrades. He saw the color of the war with all its shades. He could cite hundreds of stories about the war he painfully experienced.

Family History:

When Marvin came home from the war, he had a close relationship with Dorothy, his high school sweetheart, and had kept the letters sent between them. He had promised to marry her after he left the army. Marvin got married to Dorothy, a rather homely woman, and held a job for many years at the local supermarket as a cash register operator. She had no ambition. They had children, and it seemed at that time Marvin's mental condition started to deteriorate. Dorothy was unable to put up with his mental conditions like a lack of hygiene, poor communication, locking himself in a room for a weeks, talking to himself, and sleeplessness.

History of Illness:

Marvin and his older brother tried for the first time to seek treatment for him. He went through many clinics and several psychology assessments. He was also taking all sorts of psychotic medications for his mental condition, but became very disenchanted with the whole medical treatment for his mental illness. When he came to me, he was rather mistrusting and he closed himself up to me and would not talk. I developed a very strong rapport with him, and gradually, he started to trust me and open himself up to me.

Marvin had a vast knowledge of medicine and started to talk with me about it. For example, when he used to come for his appointment, he would sit in the waiting room and engage in conversations about the health problems of the rest of the staff in our clinic. Marvin was the one who could give them a thorough explanation and proper diagnosis of their health concerns. Every one of us in the clinic was baffled and amazed about Marvin's vast medical knowledge.

In one of our sessions, I asked him if he went to medical school. He said "Yes."

I asked, "When was that?"

He replied, "In my past life."

"Marvin, are you joking with me?"

"No," and continued, "This is why I am frustrated. No one understands that I was living this life before."

I asked, "Where?"

"In Germany."

I asked, "Where did you go to school?"

He said, "In Germany."

I asked, "Do you know the German language?"

He said, "Of course," and he started to speak the German language to me. It was a breakthrough session.

He continued, "This is my second time in the war. I was with the German army in the beginning of the Second War, and I died, then came back and went to the Vietnam War. No one understands what I am going through in my daily life. I cannot tell people because they already consider me crazy.

I said, "Marvin, allow me to verify what you just said."

He said, "You can do anything, but this is the whole truth. I was on the earth before as a doctor in Germany, trained there, died in the war, then came back, and this is why I have all the knowledge of medicine."

I decided to find out and put the pieces together to verify what Marvin had just told me. Of course, I got permission from him and maintained the confidentiality between us.

I called up his older brother, and he came to see me. I said, "Please, tell me about Marvin."

He said, "Marvin is a very fine human. He was rather aloof in his teenage years, and did not socialize much with people. He was shy in a way, did not speak a lot, and spent time by himself. Moreover, he had an incredible knowledge of medicine."

I asked if he studied medicine, and he said, "No. When he finished high school, he joined the army, came back, got married, and developed some sort of mental problem. I really did not even see him reading any books on medicine. Sometimes he told me that this life was not the only life that we live in. Perhaps, people live many lives before. I normally dismissed it, and felt that my brother was hallucinating. He is a very loving father of his children, and he wants to send his son to study medicine. He does not bother anyone, and is a very peaceful man, but he has lost all interest in life and has lost touch with reality. We are really frustrated with his mental condition, and we hope to see Marvin come back to the personality that we knew before he joined the army."

Then I called Dorothy, his ex-wife, and asked to see her. She was receptive. She came and informed me that Marvin never used his hands on her, but sometime he got angry. He did not take care of himself. He did not bathe for weeks and weeks, did not brush his teeth, and did not talk for weeks at a time. He locked himself in a room, and would not see anyone. Sometimes he did not even eat, even though he had such a vast knowledge of medicine.

I asked, "Dorothy, where did he get such knowledge?"

She said, "He told me once that he was a doctor in Germany, and I laughed at him, so he stopped saying that."

I asked, "Have you observed any unusual behavior about him?"

She said, "Yes, I have sometimes heard him talking in a different language, and I asked him about it. He said, 'This is the German language.' And I asked him when he learned the German language. 'Did they teach it to you in Vietnam?' because I have known this man since high school. Perhaps this is part of his mental illness. One day I received a letter from him when he was in Vietnam, and the letter was in the German language. I thought maybe he was just joking with me or somebody wrote it for him, but I knew his handwriting; it was from him."

She continued, "I really do not know, and even sometimes when he gets upset, he tends to curse me in that language which he called German. He did not go to school to study it, so where did he get it? I have no answer, but I must tell you, there is a clear mark in his lower abdomen. He told me that he died from this one and came back to life. I just laughed when I heard him say that. I said, 'Please, Marvin, do not say that and embarrass us in front of people.'"

I then spoke with his son and daughter, and both of them liked him very much and they thought of him as a nurturing father with a great wealth of knowledge of medicine. So, after my meetings with his family members and verifying all the pieces of information, I was convinced that I was dealing with a clear case of reincarnation.

Edgar Casey [American spiritual man] has written about hundreds of cases of reincarnation and has documented that in volumes and volumes of books. Perhaps, Marvin was a doctor, was killed, and came back to life. I shared that with him and told him that he had been reincarnated. He felt a sense of relief.

He trusted me fully and, gradually, he told me about certain events that took place in his pervious life. I worked with our psychiatrist to reduce his medications. He started to truly look forward to our sessions, and he told me all about his experiences in his past life and in the army. Perhaps, Marvin was also suffering from a case of Post-Traumatic Stress Disorder since he served in two wars, and that may have stayed in his conscious mind.

Since Marvin had complete trust in me, I used it for the advantage of treatment course. During every therapeutic session I suggested to him to do something to regain control over his life. He enrolled in the Henry Ford Community College and took basic sciences courses; he started to exercise, and he spent time with his son and daughter who were married at that time. He took a bath every day, he brushed his teeth after every meal, he took walks every day in the park next to his house and he went to Starbucks and talked to people. He also started to socialize with his ex-wife, Dorothy, and started to attend Veterans' meetings and talk about his painful experiences in the war.

Then, one day he told me that he wanted to go to Germany to put some closure on his experiences. I told him that was a fine idea, and that; perhaps, he would need to take his son with him. They went together and when they came back, his son was convinced that his father was in Germany because he went to the village where he grew up and asked about specific people; the neighbors knew them and that they had died as well.

Marvin reduced his medication. He had a cousin who worked for a

German company where he had Marvin do some manual work. The cousin informed me that they liked Marvin a lot, and he spoke with them in the German language. He did not say anything about being in Germany previously, but that he just had an interest in the language.

Marvin's life improved and he managed it to the best of his ability. He kept coming to our weekly sessions. When I informed him that I was leaving the clinic, he was truly despondent, but I transferred his case to a fellow psychologist.

The merit of this case is that this is not the only life we have on the earth. We do not die. The concept of death is a very simplistic one that science and religions are agreed upon: there is no death in a specific sense. For example, we as humans have two dominations—a physical one and a spiritual one (body and soul). When our life in the world comes to an end, the spirit roams around and may raise up until God places it somewhere, it is just a mystery. As far as our body is concerned, it tends to disintegrate to its original element, which is dirt. We say there is no death because the laws of physics tell us that our body is matter; matter cannot be destroyed, but it can be transformed into its original elements. Needless to say, the original element of our body is dirt or clay; thus, the body becomes fertilizer for the plants. Maybe the apple that you are eating right now was a breast of a beautiful Brazilian woman. Or, the tomato that you have may have come from the eyes of an evil man in Iraq. Or, the delicious plum may have come from the beautiful legs of a Swedish woman.

Thus, the concept of reincarnation is not a strange one to human thinking, but we as human beings tend to dismiss anything that our minds cannot comprehend or understand. If we do not understand things, it does not mean that it does not exist. We are very limited in our comprehension and understanding of how our own body works, let alone understanding how this vast universe operates.

If You Want to be Happy
for the Rest of Your Life
Just Find Yourself a Moroccan Wife

I was vacationing with a couple of friends in Oman and in May, 2004. My phone rang, and there on the phone was my friend, Sana, saying hello and wondering about why we had not seen each other for a couple of weeks. Normally, we were part of a group of friends who met in a different home each weekend for some food and intellectual discussion.

I said, "I am in Oman with Abu Saeed and Abu Khalid, and asked, "What is the news, Sana?"

She said, "My sister just came from Paris, she is home with me, and would you like to meet her?"

Abu Saeed over heard the phone conversation and said, "Talib, her sister will be your wife." We all laughed and thought that was a weird thought because I had never seen her, nor heard about her from Sana. He continued, "Talib, trust me. My feeling is telling me you will marry this woman."

The three of us then went for dinner and wandered around the local market in Oman. We saw a shop for local medicine for people who tended to lose their hair, but mainly for women. Abu Saeed asked me to buy the medicine.

I asked, "What is it for? I am a bald man, and I do not need to have any hair."

He explained, "Not for you. It is for your prospective wife."

I asked, "Abu Saeed, where is this premonition coming from?"

He replied, "I just feel this woman is going to be your wife and she is losing some of her hair."

And so, I bought the medicine and brought it with me to Abu Dhabi.

We returned to Abu Dhabi and, after a couple of days, I went to Sana's apartment and visited with her and her husband. Then I saw her sister who I had never seen before and I said to Sana, "You have never told me that you have such a gorgeous sister."

She said, "My sister, Safe, is living in Paris because she was married to a French man. And now, she wants to move to Abu Dhabi to live with me because she has recently gotten a divorce." We spent that evening talking until a late hour of the night, and I felt such a joyful feeling inside of me.

The next day I invited both of them for dinner and dancing because both of them loved to dance. We went to an Italian restaurant and after dinner, we went dancing. It remains vivid in my mind: Safe was wearing white trousers, and she looked just impeccable. She was an incredible dancer, and she took over the dance floor. Her dance was a mix of spiritual movement and seduction. She left everyone gasping for breath with the way she moved her body. All the people in the nightclub literally stopped dancing, fascinated with her body's movements. As I saw people watching her with such astonishment, I thought, "On the dance floor, Safe represented a Goddess from Greek mythology that held her audiences spellbound. And at that point, I felt jealous and it was as if my mind was telling me, "She will be your wife, and you have to protect her."

It was almost morning when we went home. I went to bed, but my head was spinning all night long, a stream of thoughts attacking me. The main question I had was, "Is Safe the one that I have been waiting all my life for, my soul mate?"

I started dating Safe, which meant that every day after I finished my work I went and picked her up, and we would spend time together to get to know each other. I must say, Safe was a woman with mystical qualities, and I really started to lose my ground. We traveled inside the United Arab Emirates, and we got very close to each other. Then, we had to face the inevitable decision regarding getting married.

On June 24, 2004, Safe, Sana, and I celebrated Safe's birthday and, over dinner, agreed that Safe would go back to Paris to finalize her divorce and I would go to America to take care of my things. Then, I would travel to Morocco to meet Safe's family and to formally ask for her hand.

I finished my concerns in Detroit, Michigan, July of 2004 and flew to Morocco to meet her family. Safe and her sister came to the airport to pick me up, and we went to Safe's home. There, her father, mother, and all her sisters greeted me at the doorstep with milk, rice, and dates, the tradition in Morocco for newly wed people. Safe's family are wonderful people, and they received me with such love and appreciation. We announced our marriage with the blessing of her parents and the rest of the family.

To me, the family dynamic seemed to be that of her mother was the dominant member of the family and it felt like the women in the family have the say over the men? Perhaps, that was the Moroccan culture. I stayed a few days and then went back to Abu Dhabi to be ready for the arrival of my bride, Safe.

I thought again about Abu Saeed's prediction that Safe would be my wife that night when her sister called. Neither Abu Saeed nor I were able to explain that mysterious thought. And even more mysterious was that I bought the hair medicine of Oman to give to Safe because she is losing some of her hair.

Safe came to Abu Dhabi on August 20 2004, and l was so delighted to have a partner in my life after all the years of being alone. I wanted to please her in every way. For example, one day while Abu Saeed was around, I was massaging Safe's foot. He said, "Talib, do not do that for an Arab woman because she will not respect you. You might do that for an America woman, but an Arab woman does not understand that, and she might consider it a sign of weakness and submission to her. It is not a cultural practice here." Perhaps, Abu Saeed was right, as I discovered later.

Safe invited her brother Ali to come from Morocco to live with us and find a job in Abu Dhabi. He was very much a gentleman. Life was joyful and pleasant most of the time as we shared a lot of fun and laughter.

Sex with Safe was beyond this world. It was a very spiritual connection between us. And, we could spend hours and hours talking about different subjects. She had a vast knowledge about many things in life, and she was a very helpful and stimulating individual. As the old wisdom of Confucius goes, "Who can find a good woman? She is precious beyond all things." Safe was a real gem, and she became everything to me in this world.

On September 19, 2004, exactly one month after Safe came to Abu Dhabi, I started to feel some pain in my left shoulder, and it aggravated very quickly. I visited several doctors, but to no avail. The pain became psychological and even more physical. I felt severely depressed and anxious and had crying spells. The pain became unbearable, and I even started to think about suicide. By then, I was suffering from excruciating pain, and did not know what to do. I would describe the pain as if someone had a sharp knife and was slicing my skin to pieces. I avoided walking on the Cornish of Abu Dhabi, the road next to the sea, because I was afraid of jumping in the sea and drowning myself. I lost all interest in living, with no desire for food or anything. I just cried and was unable to sleep. I talked with several of my professional friends, and all of them were bewildered; none could explain what I was suffering from. I went to work, but I had to present a persona and pretend that I was fine. I actually suffered silently for over three months.

Safe was very supportive, but she was hurt as well, and she, herself, was also in terrible pain. We were both suffering and did not know what to do. Life became meaningless to both of us. She had her own psychological difficulties, and she suffered as a result of my suffering. We were both lost in a painful condition, psychologically and physically.

Abu Saeed visited us and saw both our painful conditions, but mainly mine. He said, "Listen, Doc, I know you are a scientific man, and all of your schooling was in America, and you tend to approach life with scientific reasoning. But, in you present ordeal I want you to explore religion and see what the religious scholars may suggest for your condition."

I replied, "I have tried everything to heal myself, but to no avail," and reluctantly agreed with Abu Saeed to see a religious man.

He made a few calls, and it was suggested that I visit a religious man in Oman, well-known for his understanding of the black magic. Because everyone was telling me that I was clearly suffering from the work of the black magic, and because such work was very common in the Moroccan culture, I said, "Let me give it a try."

So, we drove to Oman, Abu Saeed, my wife, and I. We found the person we wanted walking on the beach, though none of us knew him. He motioned to his son to take us to his home. There, he lit a candle and incense, and began reading from the Holy book, the Quran. Until this point, he had not uttered a single word. Then, he turned his face to us, and with a big smile said, "How is Shama?"

I replied, "I do not know," and my wife explained, "She is my ex-mother-in-law, and she lives in Morocco."

He explained that she was the one who had done a serious work to keep us apart. It was then my wife remembered her ex-mother-in-law telling her that she would never let her stay with any man. My wife had been married to a Moroccan man before and she was married to a Frenchman, and Shama was her first husband's mother.

Then the religious man turned to face me and said, "Talib, you are non-believer in God."

I said, "Yes."

He continued, "You will never heal from your painful condition until you come close to God and have faith in his amazing power." I was shocked and baffled that he could know our names and more surprised that he could diagnose the trouble so well and so accurately.

Then, I asked him a question. "So, what can I do to heal myself from this incredible pain?"

He responded, "You must split from your wife; the work of evil that has been done on both of you is very strong, and it is impossible to stay together."

The room became silent. We both felt a deep sense of helplessness, and everyone in the room shed some tears. The religious man continued, "You also need to develop a faith and love for God, and then you can heal yourself." He looked again at my wife and said, "Safe, you are also possessed by some evil force inside of you, and you have to free yourself from these forces which have operated inside of you all these years. They will never let you be a mother or partner as long as they are in you."

What we heard during the session was astounding and unbelievable. I asked him wither there was a charge for his service, and he said," Just offer some help to the poor people that you may find on your way."

The religious man, or the pundit man, told us three things, all of them very true. One, I had spent all my life as a non-believer. Two, Safe was possessed by evil forces, and it was true. She used to stay in bed, suffering for three or four days, for no obvious reason, and she was living in constant psychological pain. Perhaps, the evil forces were operating inside of her. The third statement was that her ex-mother-in-law had worked hard to keep us apart. I thought that since the first two things he said about us were true, though he had never seen us before, then we might need to test the third hypothesis. We might have to split temporarily to see how our painful condition might feel.

We agreed that my beloved wife should spend time in Morocco, and I would see if there was any change in my painful condition. I took Safe to Dubai, and she flew Emirate Airline to Morocco on December 14, 2004. The minute I said good-by to her and left the airport, I started to feel a little bit better. A few days later the smile came back to my face, and the pain gradually began to subside. A few weeks later, I started to resume my normal life, the desire for food returned, and my sleep came back to me. I started to notice a marked improvement in my mental and physical condition. It seemed the effect of the black magic was slowly disappearing. In the meantime, I was talking with Safe almost daily, and we agreed that we had to split. But, she had to come back and try to be together again.

Safe came back in January, 2005, and I was so happy to have her again. However, the pain started again, and I felt like I wanted to just disappear from the face of the earth and put an end to the situation. Safe was understanding and compassionate toward me. She suggested that we get divorced, but remain friends.

We went to the divorce court in Abu Dhabi. Normally, according to Islamic law the man says to his wife, "I divorce you," three times, and the divorce takes place. I was not able to say it, and I went into a crying spell; Safe was the same. The judge said, 'Listen, we cannot do it. Go home for few days and come back again. It seems very difficult for both of you to split." And then he asked, "Why don't you want to get divorced? It seems to me that both of you love each other." We did not explain our situation to him, and we left the court without being able to say the divorce word.

We went back to the court the next week, and we both held each other and cried without stop. Then, I uttered the most painful words—"I divorce you"--so the court could record it. We both went home with broken hearts and feelings of helplessness in the face of what had happened to us.

Safe prepared to move out, but she had no specific plan. She found a family who knew her sister, Sana, and because Sana had moved with her husband to South Korea, the family asked Safe to stay with them for a while. I did not see her often because every time I saw her, a lot pain was stirred up inside of me. I was deeply saddened and felt there was a deep hole in my soul.

Safe was a smart woman and strong enough to move on, putting the divorce behind her. She applied to work for Emirate Airline, and she got the job. She may still be working there. I have not seen her, nor talked to her since May of 2005.

As far as my life is concerned, I am still single. I decided to date as many different women as I could, but none of them fulfilled my spiritual yearning to have a wholesome partner like Safe was. Most of my relationships are physical ones. I feel so empty when the women leave my place, but I consider it just passing time because I like sex very much. All my friends pressure me to get myself a partner, but my answer to them is "I do not believe in the traditional way of finding someone. I just leave it to the power of the universe, to serendipity, because I have been married twice, and serendipity played a major role in putting my partners on my path.

The other aspect of my life, faith, is a result of the condition that I have been through with Safe and the healing that took place inside of me. I have developed a strong faith in the loving power of the universe, what we call Almighty God. I started to see the world through my faith, and I am in complete submission to the will of God. I can go back and look over the previous years of my life and the turbulent experiences that I went through. It seems clear that God was always with me and has helped me tremendously as I sailed through the ocean of life. Now my faith sustains me and keeps me a strong spiritual individual. I am no longer depressed or anxious or angry because I "let the Ego go and let God in," as they say in AA [Alcoholic Anonymous meetings].

GUILT FEELING

It was two years ago, while I was working in Abu Dhabi, that Nadir's brother brought him for psychological treatment. The presenting problem was that he was severely clinically depressed, and no antidepressant medications had worked for him. He had not seen a psychologist before, and he refused to come to see me. The brother reported that he did not leave his room and did not want to face the world. He was living by himself. We agreed that he would come to see me on a weekly basis, so he started to come with his brother because he was unable to drive. Undoubtedly, the first few sessions were just to build rapport and a trusting therapeutic relationship.

Nadir was a 48-year-old divorced male with no children and was born in Egypt. He had come to Abu Dhabi 15 years earlier to work as a shoemaker, his trade in Egypt. Except for the previous five years, he had not worked, and his brother had supported him financially. I was trying to get him motivated to engage in the therapeutic process, and he gradually began to open up to me. I just wanted him to get out of his room and try to eat and take a bath as he had refused to take a bath. His brother had forced him to bathe after a week of negotiations because the weather in Abu Dhabi is quite hot and humid, and because a person easily sweats, the body produces an odor. Nadir had lost all desire to live and just wanted to bury himself alive. There was no eye contact and during the whole session, he bent his head down. He was very short in his answers, with no elaboration, and that can be very difficult for me because I needed to know about what lead to his profound depression. However, his brother reported that he had been fine until the death of his sister. Since then, Nadir had taken all sorts of medications, but to no avail.

After a few sessions, I saw a gleam of hope as Nadir started to trust me and open up. He told me the following story.

The three of us came to Abu Dhabi to work, my older brother, my younger sister, and myself, because our life in Egypt was very hard as far as making a living, and we could barely feed ourselves. As a family, we struggled with daily life in Cairo, and the opportunity to make a living in Egypt was very limited. Sometimes we even went a few days without earning a penny. We all had to share what we could make just to feed ourselves. Then, my older brother suggested that we go to work in Abu Dhabi. So, we came here, and I found a job in a place where I fixed or shined shoes. The three of us lived in a one-bedroom apartment. My older brother got married to his cousin in Egypt, and he had to move out of the apartment, so I stayed with my sister, Aida, who is 10 years younger than I. Our life was simple, and we were very limited in our income. My sister, Aida, started to work in a cleaning company that cleaned up after wedding parties in Abu Dhabi, and she started to make decent money.

Nevertheless, Aida wanted me to find a husband for her because she wanted to have a child, and she was 28 years old. According to the Arab traditions, a woman has to wait until a man comes to ask for her hand. Aida was crying and praying to God that she wanted to have a child before it was too late. One day she said; my brother, "Nadir, my womb is crying to have a baby." However, there was a serious problem arising with Aida. She had started to eat a lot, mainly at night, a nervous eating because she felt lonely, and she wanted to fill the void inside her with food. Although she had a pretty face, she used food to comfort herself as we sometimes do as a treatment for something missing in our life. Aida was overweight and that added to the problem that not too many suitors were interested in her. She was just eating to soothe her anxiety, and she considered herself an unlucky woman. Although she was helping herself by working, she also had such a generous spirit that she would give the shirt off her back, as the common expression goes.

She started to push me to get married so she could enjoy my children since she had lost all hope of her getting married. I found myself an Egyptian woman who lived in Abu Dhabi. My older brother's wife knew her because they worked together in a shipping company where they wrapped up furniture or merchandises and sent it all over the world. My older brother blessed the marriage since it came through his wife.

⁜ ⁜ ⁜

Nadir continued his story, and I was very attentive to his report. He continued.

⁜ ⁜ ⁜

We were three people in a one-room apartment because we could not afford the expensive rent in Abu Dhabi since our income was meager. My sister, Aida, was very sensitive, so she tended to leave the apartment most of the time so I could have time alone with my wife. Aida spent her time wandering through the Abu Dhabi malls since there was nothing else to do in Abu Dhabi, it cost money to go to movies or do something else, and since she has limited income.

Then, trouble started between me and my wife. She had a strong sexual appetite beyond my sexual ability, and she wanted to have sex three or four times a day, even though most of the time my mind was elsewhere, worrying about how to make a living. My wife's income went to her poor family in Egypt, and the problem in the Arab culture is that a man must provide for his wife in whatever she needs. After six months of marriage, my wife missed her family and wanted to spend the summer with them. I welcomed the idea because I really needed to have a break from our daily sex. She did not take into consideration my situation; she said I had to do it for her. Sometimes late at night I saw her masturbating, and I said, "All that, and not enough for you?" Perhaps, I was not lucky in my marriage--I married a nymphomaniac, and I was a man with a low sex drive. So, my wife left to return to Egypt, and I stayed with my sister, Aida, who I loved very much. I enjoyed being with her although Aida was a very unfortunate woman who became a "spinster." As a result, she was depressed and tearful most of the time.

One day the sun was very strong, and the curtain in our apartment fell down. My sister asked me to hang the curtain back up because summertime in Abu Dhabi can be very hot and temperatures can reach 50 Centigrade. I said, "Aida, I am really tired, and you can do it."

She replied, "I do not want to do it."

Then we left, and the next day Aida said, "Nadir, please put the curtain back up. The apartment is too hot."

I said, "Aida, you can do it."

She replied, "I really have a bad feeling about this curtain, and I do not feel that I am supposed to do it. You are the man of the house, and you can do it."

Then we became involved in a very heated argument over the curtain, and I refused to put it back. She said, "Brother, I am too heavy to get up and do it."

I said, "Let the dumb apartment stay hot, and I will not do it."

Then she gave me a long look and her tears rolled down. She said, "Brother, you are not helpful to me," and went to hang the curtain. She got a chair because the curtain was high and it had to be hung from the outside. She put the chair on the balcony and stood over it, holding the curtain in one hand while trying to reach the nail with her other hand. While I was watching her struggle to put the curtain back, she slipped from the chair and fell down to the street from the eighth floor of the building. I went to her, and all the neighbors went out because they had heard the slam of her body onto the ground. I saw my sister's head smashed on the concrete, her blood all over. I touched her, and there was no breath in her. The ambulance was called. She was taken to the hospital, but they found that she was already dead. We buried her the next day.

That scene is indelible in my mind, and every day I replay that record. I did not tell my brother that she had asked me to put up the curtain, and since then, the guilt feeling is eating me up inside. I was supposed to put the curtain back up, and I felt I was the cause of my sister's death. I cannot live with myself, and I cannot forgive myself for what has happened.

✢ ✢ ✢

While Nadir was telling me this story, he was crying deeply. Then, he continued.

✢ ✢ ✢

I lost all interest in this stupid life. When my wife returned from her vacation, she was initially supportive, but, again, she wanted me to have sex with her while I was barely able to function at my work. I was doing the sex as a duty, not as an enjoyable experience. Since the death of my sister, I had sunk into deep depression and had lost all interest in living, simply trying to manage my day-to-day work. When I went to work, I tended to put aside my personal feelings and pretended that I was fine. Of course, the people around me knew my situation and the loss of my sister. Every Friday I went to visit Aida's grave, and cried a lot. But, what could I do? I thought of suicide several times, but I thought God would not forgive me and would just let me live my miserable life in sheer pain.

The struggle with my wife over sex was exhausting, but she had to have it anyway. Sometimes I was not even able to get an erection because of my mental condition. She was very demanding and just wanted her needs satisfied without regard to what I went through. No doubt, the trouble escalated between us. I asked her to please give me some time to overcome the death of my sister and that I would be her man again, but she would not understand.

Sadly enough, there was another incident after the death of my sister that sliced my heart to pieces. It was the night of the Eid in 2005. Eid is a Muslim holiday celebrated after a month of fasting for Ramadan. My boss asked me to stay a few hours more to finish a job because the next day would be the Eid, and everyone wanted their shoes to be ready. So I called up my wife and told her I would be late that night.

She said, "Fine.

But then the boss changed his mind and felt sorry for keeping me for such long hours, and said, "Nadir, it is unfair for you to be away from your family, so just go home." So I did.

I went home and when I approached my apartment, I heard some laughter inside. To my painful astonishment, when I opened the apartment, I found my wife and another man with her, totally naked, making love on the couch. There was alcohol on the table. When they saw me, they rushed to the other room and put on their clothes. The man left and she went to the room and closed the door behind her. Then, she opened the door, and looked at me, and asked, "Why didn't you call me before you came?" While all this happened, I was unable to utter a single word, I was speechless, and I was totally numb. It was late at night. The next morning, she put her clothes in the luggage and left the apartment. I have not heard from her since then, and that was three years ago.

✢ ✢ ✢

"I did not tell my brother about the incident, and I have not told any other human, except for you right now, Doc."

Nadir looked at me with a somber look and said, "Doc is that enough for any man to be depressed? You are the only one to whom I have told the whole story of my sister's death and my wife's infidelity." Nadir continued saying, "I do not know about my wife or where she has been for over three years. I did not tell my older brother about the two incidents. I am keeping everything in my heart, and I cannot take it anymore. The only salvation for me now is death. It has been four years since the loss of my sister, and my wife left over three years ago. I have left my work. I am no longer working, and my older brother supports me financially. I have lost the will to live. I do not even see the sun or the moon; I just stay in my room. I take all these medications, but so far none has helped me.

I paused and took a deep breath, then looked at Nadir and said, "My heart is with you, and I truly feel very sad about your case." I said, "Nadir, I understand all the guilt that you have over the loss of your sister and the deception of your wife, but can you give me the chance to work with you and try to help you out just to live a functional life?

He said, "Doc, I understand your sincerity, but I am very clear about what I want, I do not want to live this life any more. My life is meaningless, with no enjoyment at all, so what is the point of living?"

I replied, "Nadir, there is no amount of guilt or regret that will undo what has happened. You may need to learn acceptance of things that can happen in our lives, and that there are certain things that we have no control over."

He said, "Doc, you try to bring logic into my situation. There is no logic here. My guilt feeling is controlling me, and the two incidents are hard for me to digest."

I said, "Nadir, ending one's life is not a solution, but is a coward's act.

It is running away from the inevitable. Things can go wrong in life, and we need to face that with some courage."

He responded, "Doc, you try to bring rational thinking here, but the whole existence of the human race is irrational, and I am a bad person. That is why this has happened to me; thus, I do not deserve to live by any means."

From an ethical standpoint, I called his brother and informed him about Nadir's desire to die. I insisted that his brother had to be watched in any medical setting.

Brother said, "Doc, he refused to be in any hospital."

I said, "Then you need to have someone watch him because he may hurt himself, and it seems he means it."

Nadir came to see me sporadically. When he sat in the sessions, he just wanted to talk, and I allowed him to ventilate. He told me that he liked to come to our sessions. I also worked to shift his perception from dying to an appreciation of living. Then one day, all of the sudden, his brother called me and said that he wanted me to come to Nadir's funeral. Nadir had jumped from the same balcony from which his sister fell and died right away.

The merits of the case are these. Guilt feelings can ferment inside of us and become unbearable; thus, we need to be aware of such feelings and not let them rest inside our soul because they tend to rear their heads whenever certain situations present themselves or remind us of situations. Nadir clearly felt that he was the cause of his sister's death. Thus, he directed the guilt towards himself and ended his life in the same way his sister died.

Also, he felt he was a worthless human being, especially when his wife went with another man. Undoubtedly, she put her own needs above the wellbeing of her husband. Therefore, sexual compatibility is very essential to the survival of a marriage. It is suggested that in the beginning of any relationship, a couple needs to understand each other sexually and the means of their satisfaction so that the marriage can be enjoyable, rather than a constant struggle which is what happened in Nadir's case.

Another element of disturbance in this case is poverty. Nadir's family was very poor and that made their life extremely difficult. Life can be very hard in the Arab world as a result of poverty. While the area sits on enormous wealth, the biggest portion of the Arab population is poor, and these people have their own brand of pathology. Poverty can breed all kinds of psychological and mental disturbance. For example, a poor individual may feel insecure, angry, anxious, or depressed and suffer from poor self-image, worthless, and most of all, a dehumanized feeling. It is also shown that poverty tends to flirt with the dark side of the soul. Therefore, we all have a moral obligation to eradicate poverty if we really want to have a dignified people who are productive and creative. Moreover, we may need to place a global focus on the mental health issue and establish it as a priority. The sad reality is that the mental health services in the Arab world are limited and of a very narrow scope.

Other observations include those related to Aida's case. She represents a sizable number of Arab females who are near or past the age of 30 and are not married. Technically, the Arab term for this type of woman is "spinster," and to be considered a "spinster" can be devastating to a large portion of the female population. It can breed all sorts of psychological difficulties. Once a female reaches a certain age and she has no male companion, she feels depressed, anxious, and most of all, angry at the society that deprived her of the natural pleasures of sex and bearing children. Although the Arab man can have multiple sexual relationships, the Arab female cannot. She is the bearer of the family honor, and she has to stay a virgin until she gets married. No doubt, this is a double standard. Thus, Arab women are at a disadvantage, and this can have social ramifications for the whole society. Perhaps one of the reasons why Arab women do not find husbands is that Arab men are unable to support a family due to the poverty that has infected a large section of the population. Another reason may be the norm for the society regarding female sexuality. For example, Aida had to wait for the man to come along, and if he did not come, she had to live by herself and stay home. That can be a very stifling and suffocating life for any human.

In addition, Aida had a premonition, a bad feeling about the curtain, and even told Nadir that she was not happy about it. The human soul can sense something that might happen beforehand, and she did.

PSYCHOLOGY OF ADAM STORY

When Almighty God created Adam and put in him the spirit of life, perhaps his intention was to look at his marvelous creation and see His ultimate beauty and miracle in one creature. Then, God instilled in his newly created man the malicious intents which were greed, envy, jealousy, aggression, and poor self -control. God also put in him the benevolent intents which are love, kindness, creativity, compassion, and motivation to make the world a better place for his fellow man. And man stayed by himself and looked around and found that he was lonely. He went to God complaining, "Please, God, I cannot stay by myself. I am terribly lonely."

God found Adam's request reasonable and created Eve so he could have companionship. But, once Eve arrived, his life was changed drastically and forever. She animated his life. Adam was delighted to see Eve around him, and she asked him to make love to her. He was not familiar with such pleasure, so she showed him how to do it. Then, he freaked out and went out of his mind. He proclaimed, "This is so breath taking and tantalizing!" And Eve said, "Anytime we make love, we are a happy couple, newly discovering our new life in Heaven.

Adam and Eve took a walk around Heaven and smelled the flowers and sampled all the varieties of fruits and vegetables. Of course, there were no animals, so basically our parents, Adam and Eve, were vegetarian. They lived very healthy lives. Then jealousy started to develop in the other creatures around them in Heaven, and the creatures wondered why in the world God had given this couple such privileges. "What do they have that we do not have?" they asked. Clearly, they had observed God's preferential treatment of the couple.

Then God sensed what had transpired among the inhabitants of Heaven and called for a general meeting. There were three tribes in Heaven--the tribe of Angels, the tribe of the Devil, and the new tribe of Humankind. God said, "Listen, folks, I have created all of you, and I know you very well. I just created a new tribe, and I prefer this one over all of you. And the reason for that is because I took part of the angel's characteristics and part of the Devil's characteristics, and put both in the newly created man. This is why I prefer them over all of you. Moreover, I want you all to salute Adam and Eve as newly created creatures and my favorite ones."

Of course, the angels stood up and saluted them, but the Devil Tribe stood up and said, "My Almighty God, we will never salute them because you created them from clay, and we are created from fire. And fire is far better than clay." Here they presented to God a serious case of discrimination.

God said, "I order you to salute Adam and Eve."

The tribe of devils replied, "God, we have great respect and love for you, but we really feel that we are better than them. And, we are going to prove to you that we will even have control over them. Can you please give us the opportunity to work with the new tribe? We will seduce them and show you that those people are false and are not even true to themselves." They begged God to give them until Judgment Day to show everyone who was better.

So, God granted the Devil Tribe the new privileges. Then, God who had all the mercy and love for the new creatures asked for a private meeting with Adam and Eve without involvement of any of the others. He said, "Listen carefully. I created you and prefer you over all those creatures, but I need to warn you that my intention when I created you was for you to be around me in Heaven and not leave my sight. You are my favorites. However, there is a caveat that the Devil Tribe is intending to seduce you and make your lives miserable ones, and that means disobeying me. And, if you do that, you will be out of this place heaven, you will be disgraced, and you will really suffer. Then, God repeated the message and asked, "Are you clear and aware of the danger that surrounds you, that you will face serious cases of challenge?"

"Of course," they replied. "We will obey you in whatever you order us to do."

God continued, "Then I will put you to the test and find out. Try to eat from all these trees, but do not eat the fruit of the pomegranate. Please, do not fail the test."

They said, "No, we are confident that we like it here and love the privileges that you have given us."

God repeated, "Eat from all the fruits and everything that I created for you, except of this tree. Please, do not even get close to it."

They said, "The message is very clear."

And God said, "If you do it, the consequences will be beyond what you can imagine, and it can be detrimental." Then God continued, "Listen well. The Devil Tribe is your enemy, and they will try to seduce you and suggest to you to take the wrong actions. Try not to listen to them at all."

They replied, "God, we are not stupid enough to lose all these privileges. We will never fail your trust in us."

They kept wandering around Heaven, enjoying everything that God put in their usage. The Devil Tribe watched them carefully and planned to seduce them by any means. The Devil Tribe was very conniving, sly, and manipulative by nature.

The couple continued to enjoy their new life, discovering everything in Heaven, sampling all the fruits and vegetables. However, the other tribes noticed a marked change in Adam's behavior since Eve came into his life and wondered what she had brought to change his life. It seemed to the rest of Heaven's inhabitants that Adam tended to act weak and funny around her, and sometimes even lost his personality. Then the Devil Tribe knew the reason and told the rest of Heaven's inhabitants. She had a vagina. "What is that?" they asked.

The Devil Tribe explained, "A vagina is an organ in Eve's body that is considered to be the source of all pleasure in the entire universe."

Of course, the Angel Tribe was not familiar with such a pleasure, but the Devil Tribe knew it well.

After seven days, one member of the Devil Tribe went to Adam and Eve and said, "Listen, why do you not eat from this tree?"

They said, "Our Almighty God said, 'Do not even touch it.'"

The Devil said, "The reason that God prevents you from eating it is because if you eat from this tree, you will live forever and have all of Heaven for you alone."

Now, you could see that the greed urge started to work in Adam and Eve. Then the Devil said, "Listen well. God is not around, and you can eat right now." Of course, they were not aware that God could see everything in this world.

Adam was hesitating, so the Devil asked Eve, "Listen, why he is that way?"

She said, "I will talk to him. He will do anything just to please me, even though he might lose his soul for me."

Here, the Devil observed that Eve had serious influence over Adam. She asked him to eat, and both of them ate from the forbidden tree.

Suddenly, the tree's leaves started to fall down over them, and there was like a thunder noise in Heaven. The couple felt terrible! God spoke. "Why did you do that? I told you the Devil will try to seduce you. I warned you, but eventually you ate from the forbidden tree. You did not wait even seven days. You have acted impulsively; I am very disappointed in you. I gave you all privileges, and that was not enough for you. I am even surprised at how much greed you have. And you are now defiant of my order. My judgment is that you go down to the earth."

They asked, "God, what is earth?"

God said, "Earth is a place where you will suffer, you will be the enemy of each other, you will see the cruelty of each other, and you will witness the injustice that you will inflict on each other." Then God continued, "Listen, there will be another hope that you will come back here."

They asked, "How can that be?"

God said, "If you try to follow my instructions which I will have for you, you will come back to Heaven, and you live here forever. But, if you disobey my earthly instructions, you will come back, but to a different place called Hell which you have not yet seen."

They went down to the earth, and they started a new life on the planet.

They gave birth to two sons, Cain and Able. Then these brothers started to feel jealous of each other. Cain said to his brother, Able, "I do not want to share the earth with you."

Able said, "Brother, it is large enough for both of us, and more."

"No. I feel I want to kill you," replied Cain.

Able said, "I will not participate in this."

Then, one day while Able was sleeping, Cain came and smashed Able's head with a big rock, and Able died. Cain did not even know how to bury him in the ground, so God sent a bird to teach him how to bury his brother. Then Cain felt miserable and regretted that he had killed his brother, but it did not matter because he was a murderer now by the law of God. He went about his normal life. He got married and multiplied and populated the earth with his offspring so that we have come from our Father, Cain, the murderer.

God began to watch and see the chaotic world of humans and said, "I do not want to leave them hurting each other, so I will send people to them to teach them the basic rules of living peacefully with each other." So, God sent many prophets to teach people how to be humane with each other. Some of the prophets failed because of the defiant nature of people, and some succeeded and some of them were killed. People did not want to accept them and did not want to see a change. God sent numerous prophets to teach the people and to deliver the message that God wanted to bring them back to Heaven. God's message was clear: life on the earth is a temporary one, and the eternal life is in Heaven next to Him.

But, mankind has refused all the rational arguments of God and has preferred to just be on the earth, enjoying the limited time that they have here. Man has gone too far in his brutality and savagery toward one another, has shed a lot of blood, and has committed the most horrible of crimes, destroying the planet without regard. Needless to say, God is watching us and feeling that He never intended seeing such brutality from His creatures.

The psychological observations of this story of Adam are these. First, Adam had a defiant nature and impulsive in his action, even when it was detrimental to his own good. Second, Adam felt lonely and wanted to have a companion. His heart yearned for a union with something beyond himself, so God created Eve. She was his salvation. This is why we saw that he tended to lose his personal strength when Eve was around him. She had power over him, and he had no power over her because he tended to be a slave to her organ, her vagina, the seat of pleasure. He tended to act funny around her, and sometimes he became hostile just to prove that he was a man. Another observation is that greed could be a prime motivation for his behavior, even though he has lost a lot in between. Mankind is very shortsighted and does not look far ahead when it comes to personal greed. Yet another observation is that aggression is embedded in the nature of man, and he does not know how to channel it or put it to a positive use. He was also impatient and did not allow enough time to find out why God prevented him from eating from that specific tree.

Here a question must be asked. Why did God send all those prophets into the world? The answer is a simple one. God considered this life of ours on the planet Earth as a short one, and it is a rehearsal for the eternal life. There is a sifting process which takes place during this limited life on earth to separate the good from the bad. The bad one will pay a heavy price, and the consequences are surely not romantic. At the same time, the good one will be very well rewarded and live through eternity in peace and joy next to God.

However, mankind is fabulously stupid because he/she prefers immediate gratifications over long-term fulfillment. They are driven by irrational thoughts and inner fears even though God has clearly shown us the way and has assured us that if we follow the path that He has designed for us, we will gain and have eternal life. If we follow the path of short pleasure or desire, we will lose. Mankind has chosen the path of losing over the path of gaining. Mankind has chosen the path of hate over the path of love (the path of love is the God pathway). Moreover, mankind's selfishness has destroyed the universe and generated wars, starvation, diseases, and injustice. Our earth "has enough for human needs, but not enough for man's greed," as Gandhi put it.

God showed great wisdom when He wove two opposing forces into the fabric of man, good and bad--to give him the ability to differentiate; the freedom to manifest his humanity; to animate his life, rather than live the stoic life of the angel or the lustful life of the devil; and the power to choose and transcend. When Adam and Eve descended from Heaven down to the earth God specifically asked them to make the earth like Heaven. Unfortunately, their offspring have unconsciously inherited from them all the dysfunctional qualities. Those dysfunctional qualities are greed, aggression, envy, jealousy, poor self- control, selfishness, lust, and hostility. However, they have also inherited the benevolent qualities of love, kindness, compassion, creativity, and the motivation to build.

It seems obvious to the inhabitants of our earth that the dysfunctional qualities of mankind are the prevailing ones. This is why we have to be mindful that one day we will leave this short life of ours, and the challenge is this: that we must leave the earth in a better condition than when we arrived.

THE TRIUMPH OF EVIL

I moved from Detroit, Michigan to Abu Dhabi in 2002 to work as a clinical psychologist. The first thing that I did was to open a banking account so I could mange my finances. I went to the Abu Dhabi National Bank, and the lady working in the bank was very friendly, and she said, "Welcome to Abu Dhabi." We engaged in small talk, and she asked me if my family was with me.

I said, "No, I have no family. I am a single man.

She asked, "Why don't you have a woman in your life?"

I laughed and said, "Do you have one for me?"

"Yes," she said, "as a matter of fact I have my best friend who is divorced and a great person to know." She continued, "Once you have free time, you must stop by the Abu Dhabi Commercial Bank and talk to my friend by the name of Hiyam. She works in the visa section."

So, one day I went there and introduced myself as a customer who wanted to get a visa card. I saw Hiyam, a serious woman, working very diligently. She was a very attractive woman in her early- to mid-30s with dark eyes and brown hair. She was a very elegant lady and dressed in a rather conservative style. After many phone calls, she found out that I was not interested in a visa card, but I was interested in her. I invited her for coffee, and she was receptive. Then I invited her for lunch, and she was responsive. We started to talk with each other almost daily, and we became very close friends.

Hiyam became very close to my heart and I felt that she was a one-of-a-kind woman. Perhaps many of our friends wondered why we were not involved romantically since we both were single and we had no one in our lives. There were two reasons. The first one was related to Hiyam in that she was very conservative in her values and she did not believe in sex outside of marriage at all. The second reason related to me. I was always attracted to the woman who was similar to my mother physically and Hiyam does not look like my mother. We had cultivated a wonderful, supportive and meaningful friendship, and I truly cherished Hiyam to the fullest of my soul.

Oftentimes I saw Hiyam depressed, and sometimes I saw her just deeply disappointed. She always complained of insomnia. After our relationship had matured enough, I asked her, "Hiyam, please tell me what is the matter with you."

She responded, "Talib. My story is a long one, and we need specific time to talk about it." So, we set up a time for an evening, and we went to the coffeehouse. She began.

✛   ✛   ✛

My father met my mother in Palestine, and they got married. As a young couple, they moved to Jordan, but at that time, job opportunities in Jordan were slim. Then, they moved to Abu Dhabi, but my father did not find a job in Abu Dhabi, so he went to work in Libya as an accountant. He left my mother with six children; five girls and one boy. Some of us were born in Jordan, and some were born in Abu Dhabi and I am the oldest one among my siblings.

My father used to come to visit us once every four or five months. Then, during one of his trips to Jordan he was crossing the street and got hit by a car. He died right away. I was 12 years old, and though I really did not see much of my father, he was such a wonderful man and I was his favorite's daughter. His death was a trauma in my life. I lost my father, so we stayed under the supervision of my uncle, the brother of my mother. Then, my uncle developed cancer, and he died soon after my father. The management of the family was left to my mother, even though she was a young and inexperienced woman.

My older brother found a job in the Abu Dhabi municipality, and I found a job in the bank as an accountant, following in the footsteps of my father. Then, one day a man came from the refugee camp in Lebanon and asked for my hand. We thought that perhaps we needed to get to know the man, so I became engaged to him and then we went out several times. I found out that he was a very angry man and could be verbally abusive. I told my mother about him, and she said, "Daughter, just give him a chance. Once he marries you, he will be fine."

I said, "Mother, I have to trust my hunch. This man is a miserable person with no regard for anything."

She replied, "Daughter, God sent him, and you have to accept your lot in life. People can change." Normally, the Arab culture believes that a woman can tame the man.

So, we got married, though I was crying on my wedding day. People thought that my tears were tears of joy, but in reality they were tears of pain thinking I was going to be married to such abusive man.

We moved from our house, and he found an apartment for us. I saw him come in very late at night, and I asked him, "What kind of job do you have that you have to stay so late?" He never gave me a straight answer about his job, but just kept it secret. At that time I did not make anything of it because the old-fashioned man in the Arab culture is not supposes to tell his wife about his income. When he came home late, he would wake me up and keep me entertaining him until morning. I had to work in the morning at the bank, but I used to stay with him all night long, and if I got tired and fell asleep, he beat me up. His physical and verbal abuse escalated.

I went to my mother and told her about it, and her answer to me was, "Daughter, the good Arab woman has to be patient with her husband."

I explained, "Mother, the situation is unbearable."

She just said, "Daughter, once he gets used to you, he will change." She was a woman who believed in "until death do us part."

One day he beat me up so badly that the neighbor interfered and took me to the hospital. By that time I was pregnant, and even I, myself, thought I had to stay in the marriage because I did not want my son to grow up without a father. However, the abuse continued unabated. I learned that he was abused by his family, and he was taking revenge on me as in an abuse syndrome cycle. I became the object of his abuse and aggression.

Then, I delivered Hamad, and I was so delighted that I had a son, the fruit of my miserable marriage. Hamad became my whole world. I was patient, but it seemed nothing worked with my husband. Then, one day after a year of marriage, I took my son and went back to my family. I filed for divorce.

My husband was furious, and then the real abuse began. He wanted to take custody of my son. We went to the courts for over five years, and every time he produced all sorts of documents against me. All of the documents were forged, and he paid people money to get them for him. He wanted to prove that I was an unfit mother to have the custody of my son. He even brought a report from a doctor indicating that I had physically abused my son. That would not have happened by any stretched of the imagination. I had to go to another doctor and have him examine my son. The doctor examined him and wrote a report to the court saying that there were no signs of abuse on the body of the child. But, the Judge did not accept my doctor's report, but rather accepted that of my husband's doctor who had never even seen my son. I continually asked the Judge to please look at the authenticity of those reports and documents, but he never looked into it. Anything that came from my ex-husband was accepted, and anything that came from me was rejected in the court. It seemed that I was fighting an uphill battle.

I always wondered why my ex-husband had such influence on the court and the whole legal system. I finally learned the bitter fact of life that my husband worked as a high-class pimp. He brought girls to the people who he wanted to help him. Normally, pimps in the Arab world had a lot of money, and they made the wheel go around fast. And now I figured out why I lost every single trial of the custody.

After five years of constant struggle and agony, the judge announced his verdict--the custody of my child was awarded to his abusive father. The scene in the court was unbearable. He came and grabbed my son from my hands while my son was crying and saying, "I need my mother. I do not want you." Hamad was five years old. As far as I was concerned, my feet were unable to carry me after losing my son from my hands, and I collapsed in the courtroom, breathless. I heard the judge saying, "Do not bother with her. That is a woman's way to gain sympathy."

Then someone gave me a hand and stood me back on my feet. I looked at the judge and said to him, "Your Honor, you know very well that your verdict was unfair and baseless, and I ask God to deprive you of your own child the way that you have deprived me of my child."

"God will not listen to you," he said.

I said, "He will." And I saw my son vanish before my eyes.

I left the courtroom, despondent, helpless, angry, and weak. Everything had literary come to a complete stop inside me, even my tears were frozen in my eyes. Where could I go now? I went to the Abu Dhabi seaside road and sat on a bench, looking at the waves of the sea and to the sky. I cried, and asked God several question "God, did you really intend to create such evil people? Why? Just to hurt us? God you are loving. Why are your children so cruel and mean? God, you are fair. Why are your people just pure ugly? God, I am a woman who just wanted to live peacefully with my child. I never committed any sin. I do not deserve all this pain. God, they took my child from me, and they hurt me so much. God, I am weak now and helpless. What can you do to soothe my excruciating pain? God, it is your intention that we all live with each other in harmony, so why is there so much disharmony among your children? God, I am a victim of a culture that has no regard for a woman. God, you took my father from me while I was a child, and now my son is gone. I am childless, a single woman trying to find a place in this cruel inhuman world of ours. While I was having this philosophical dialogue with God, I felt my body grow numb. I had nothing more to say or do.

The next day I left my work in the bank. I was gone for six months because I was unable to concentrate. My ex-husband took my son to the refugee camp in Lebanon, so I went to visit my Hamad there, but my ex-husband did not allow me to see him. I went to the court in Lebanon and filed for custody and visitation, but I found out the legal system in Lebanon was in shambles as well. So, I thought I could go to Jordan because it was my country and file for visitation and custody there. To my astonishment, the legal system in Jordan did not do anything to help me either.

I could see that I had lost the battle in all three countries, and I left with no options, just the mercy of my evil ex-husband. Then, suddenly, I heard that my ex-husband had taken my son and left for America. He was applying for an immigrant visa and it seemed he got it. I went to his family and asked them for his phone number in America, just to call my son. They refused to give me, and I have not talked to or seen my son for over 17 years.

Two moths after the verdict, I heard that the judge had lost his only son in a car accident, so I went to the court and I said, "Your Honor, I just came to give you my condolences, and I want to say that God has listened to me. You have lost your only son, and I have lost my only son. We are even."

The judge said, "Hiyam, do not leave. I want to talk to you." He closed the chamber and continued, "Hiyam, listen to me carefully. Every time your case came for trial, I received numerous calls from very influential people who told me not listen to this woman. It seemed that your ex-husband had a lot of clout. As you know, Hiyam, I am afraid of losing my job. I am from Mauritania, and if I do not listen to these people, they will terminate my work. This is my livelihood, and I have a family to support."

I replied, "Yes, Judge, my ex-husband was a pimp, and he used to bribe those people with women and money. That is why he won the case."

Then the judge apologized a lot. "I really feel terrible inside," he said, "but what could I do? It was either my job or your case."

❖   ❖   ❖

Now Hamad is 22 years old. I am sure he is a young man. I would love to hear his voice or even receive an e-mail from him, but I learned that his father has placed complete control over his contact with me and has censored all his movements.

During those 17 years of not hearing from my son or seeing him, many desperate thoughts came to my mind. One thought was that I would write to Hilary Clinton and asks her, as a woman, to help me out, so that I might see my son or even talk to him because the whole legal system in the Arab world has failed me. The second thought was that I would seek to visit America and try to go to my son's school so I can see him, but I did not know where he was. I only knew that he was living in California.

Sometimes, I look at my mother and think, "Mother, my hunch at that time about this man was correct--my ex-husband was an evil man--but the pressure from you forced me to marry him." Then, when I came back to my senses and thought, "What is the point of bringing up the past? Just live with what has happened and may God reward me with something else."

Hiyam had finished telling me her story, and I was speechless, angry at the legal system in the Arab world, and disappointed at the whole culture that had no sense of fairness to grant Hiram a visit with her son.

The merit of this story, no doubt, that there are evil people in the world who just want to hurt others, with no regard of any human consideration. The other observation is that women in the Arab culture are not treated fairly. Of course, the Arab may be offended and say, "No, we treat our woman very well, even better than the West." But, that is hogwash. The legal system in the Arab world needs an overhaul. Hiyam is an unfortunate woman, and there are people who are merely unfortunate. However, Hiyam was also a very strong woman who fought a long battle to get her son and did not give up. Of course, that has drained her emotionally and financially, but she held her self very high and challenged the corrupted legal system in the Arab world.

Yearning for the Union

There is an Indian myth which states that when God created Adam and Eve, they were joined together in one body. After Adam and Eve committed the grave mistake of eating of the forbidden fruit from the pomegranate tree [not the apple tree], God condemned them and sent them down to the earth. But, before they left Heaven, God split them into two pieces, a man and a woman. So, when they came down, each part started to franticly search for the other part. Thus, we as human beings spend all our life seeking the missing part of us, which we call our soul mate or partner, or the other half. Some of us get lucky, and we find the other part. But, the majority of us spend most of our life looking for the missing part we may never find. That is one of the human dilemmas, and it has caused us tremendous suffering.

In July, 2009, I traveled to Morocco to spend some time in my favorite city, Marrakesh, and, out of my love for the city, I purchased an apartment in a magnificent part of the city. Normally, in the evening, I take a walk on Mohammad V Street. Because the weather in the city is very hot in the summertime, the city comes to life in the evening and night, rather than during the day. I was strolling and looking at people and was watching how human beings present themselves in public places. I turned and saw two women waiting for a taxi. Immediately, something told me to talk to them.

I said "hello" and struck up a conversation with them. They were receptive to me, and I made them laugh. As it happened, we were all walking near my place, and I asked them to have some tea with me in my apartment. They accepted my invitation, and we went to my place.

I offered them tea and olives, which I love very much, and we started to talk about our personal lives. However, I had developed an immediate and keen interest in one of them, Awatif, and asked to see her the next day. She was receptive. They both left that night, but her image had captured my mind for the rest of the night. I hoped she would call me the next day, and I would be able to see her.

Awatif called up and came over the next day. When I saw her, she evoked something inside of me. I wanted to literally hold her and kiss her endlessly, which I did. She was very surprised with such a greeting. We went out and had dinner, and when we returned, I did not hesitate to ask her to have sex, but she said, "It is too soon, and we need to know each other." Normally, I like first to know a woman sexually and then get to know the other part of her life. I need to get the sex out of the way, and then my mind becomes clear for the rest. Lo and behold, the next day we had sex, and she moved in to live with me in my apartment.

The following night, Awatif could not sleep because she had a toothache, so I took her to the dentist who fixed her teeth. She felt very good towards me, but she did not understand the amount of attention that I was giving her. She even invited a couple of her friends to come over and see me and see how much I enjoyed being with her.

By then, I was deeply in love, or infatuation, or whatever it is called, with Awatif. I kissed her on the mouth. Normally, I do not kiss a woman unless I love her. I consider a kiss on the mouth more intimate then sex. Every night we got together and she would tell me about her life in detail. Even though she did not finish high school, she was interested in philosophical explanations to human behavior. Then, I would hold her all night long and wished that I could get under her skin. I was intoxicated with the smell of her body and her hair, I was captivated with the way she carried herself, and I was spellbound with her total being. In other words, I had lost it, and I wanted to give her everything, just to make her happy. I can describe Awatif in one sentence and that is that she is the manifestation of God's miracle of beauty, the Goddess of Beauty.

Awatif grew up in a very poor family, the only daughter among four sons. In spite of her family's poverty, they gave her anything she wanted. In other words, Awatif was a pampered girl. She married, but her husband cheated on her. She did some modeling, and she got a lot of attention from others, so she expected the world to treat her that way. I was suffering silently and told her several times that she was not a giving person. She agreed with me. She promised herself that she would change, but she was unable to do so because all of her behaviors had been ingrained in her personality. In her case, change was very difficult.

Awatif evoked two things inside of me. One was my yearning for that union with the missing part spoken of in the Indian myth, a very strong motivation for our behavior, according to Erich Fromm. And, the second was that she communicated with the image of my mother inside me, according to our beloved father, Freud. As they say, during the entire nine months in our mother's womb, we try to get out of it; and then we spend the rest of our life trying to go back inside of it. Men tend to search for their mother from whom we were separated at birth. Even Carl Jung considers the trauma of birth to be the first trauma we go through as humans. Awatif looked exactly like my mother, and once I saw her, I frantically ran to unite myself with her.

Because of the poverty and lack of education, Awatif grew up in unhealthy surroundings. Thus, she came into our relationship with lots of dysfunctional behavior. Her ex-husband cheated on her, and that had traumatized her. She did not trust men, in general, and I felt that I had to defend myself all the time. She also suffered from bouts of depression, she was easily irritated, and she said many hurtful things to me. Initially, I made excuses for her, saying that she would get used to me and change. But when I talked with her mother, she reported that Awatif's behaviors had been going on for such for a long time and that even she was frustrated with Awatif. Awatif was a very demanding and not a giving individual. She very often wanted to spend inordinate amounts of time in front of her mirror, and every other sentence she spoke she said, "I am a beautiful woman." She was a narcissistic person and was inconsiderate of others' needs. Normally, a woman who does some modeling will often become very self-absorbed; because, she is the center of attention and that can be poisonous to her soul. Thus, most of the models are not successful in relationships.

Even with all her flaws, I went through with our engagement. We invited people to attend the engagement party, complete with a musical band. I was in temporary insanity, going with the flow, and did not understand that this relationship could be disaster to me. Then, the day before my departure from Marrakesh, she said a lot of hurtful things to me. She got very angry at me, and at that moment I woke up. "Enough of this abuse" I said. "This relationship is very bad for my soul, and I am really crazy to get married this fast without even knowing her very well."

In analyzing what happened, I saw that we as human beings tend to search for our missing part and we may find it, or may never find it. As far as I am concerned, I have not found it yet. In addition, there are certain people who evoke some hidden issues in our conscious mind. We often want to attach to them, and even though we know that such an attachment or attraction can be very detriment to our soul, we pursue it anyway. It is like in the old story of a man who went to his wife and said, "I feel I am a chicken," and his wife took him to a psychologist to help convince him that he was a man, not a chicken. The psychologist said to the wife, "Leave him with me, and I will try to convince him that he is not a chicken." The wife replied, "Do not convince him otherwise." When the psychologist asked "Why?" she said, "Because we need the eggs." The merit of the story is that even when we know a relationship is absurd, we still need it.

Awatif was not equipped to have a serious relationship. She did not have the skills or the tools to make a relationship move forward. She thought I would be with her for the rest of our lives because she had experienced the incredible attention that I had given her without any reservation. The last day with her I told her that perhaps we were not meant for each other, but she disagreed. She did not accept the fact that the relationship was very sick.

I flew back to Abu Dhabi, but it seemed she was resilient enough to overcome our separation. Again, narcissistic people do not handle rejection well, but they move quickly out of relationships.

The merit of the story that man is a visual species, so beauty can captivate us, even though it can be harmful. Moreover, we as humans can sometimes go through temporary insanity, which I did. Relationships require many skills to manage it, and most of us have no such skills. The valuable suggestion, that we may need to teach relationship skills in the school system, and then we can safeguard many anguish souls.

WEDNESDAY EVENING DISCUSSION

For the past three years, the three of us, Abu Ahmed, Khalid, and I, met every single Wednesday evening from eight to ten. We also traveled together, having developed such a wonderful friendship and camaraderie. Our meeting place was the Marina Mall, upstairs in the Gerald Coffee house, in Abu Dhabi, United Arab Emirates. Usually, at the beginning of our meeting we tended to ask each other how the week had gone and each one of us reported what had happened on a personal level. Then, we moved to the serious discussions, and they tend to come up spontaneously in the form of questions, or inquiries, or observations. Any one of us might initiate the discussion, and we tended to go very thoroughly into the issues.

The discussions covered a wide range of issues, from physical health to world politics, but the focus was mainly on the concepts of living and understanding how we, as human beings, function in our lives. We all immensely enjoyed the discussion, as they could be very enlightening and entertaining. Nevertheless, we were coming from different backgrounds and educational training. Abu Ahmed was a retired career diplomat; Khalid was an attorney by training, and I, a psychologist. Thus, the inquiries would be tackled from many angles. We also recorded most of our discussions. The presentation below includes selections of the different topics that were discussed during those three years.

✤   ✤   ✤

One evening during the month of September, 2009, Khalid arrived very frustrated with his close friend and said to us, "Listen, Folks. What do we mean by friendship? Today I was very disappointed in my close friend who I thought the world of. Today he turned out to be an absolute jerk."

Abu Ahmed said, "Since I have experience in this area and am a diplomat, I have seen all kinds of people. I would say that friendship is a very essential part of our survival and existence as a human being, and we cannot live by ourselves. Friendship is an indispensable part of our relationship to the world around us. There are two kinds of friendship--the fair-weather friendship and the true friendship."

Abu Ahmed continued to discuss what that meant. "The fair-weather friend is one who just wants to be with you as long as the time is sweet, but, if you run into some troubles and you need them, you never can find them. When your situation is good and well, they are around you, but if you have difficulty and you need them, then they evaporate from the scene. Undoubtedly, that can leave a bitter taste in your mouth, and you feel disappointed. But, as David Buss, the evolutionary psychologist, notes, as part of the adapted behavior of our species, "we are greedy, and we want all things only for ourselves". If we feel our friends need some help, we think, 'Why should we help?' Yes, we might help if we check our ulterior motive. If there is personal gain or benefit, then we may help out, but if there is no personal gain, then normally we do not help. On the other hand, we enjoy seeing others suffer because that gives us an edge over them. It is a malevolent part of our human nature."

I said, "Abu Ahmed, you are drawing an ugly picture of friendship."

He continued, "They are your friends as long as you are fine, but once you need them, they will run away, and you will never see them again. Or, they may switch off their phone." Switching off or not answering the phone is a mechanism that is used in the Middle East to avoid talking to people because people are not assertive enough to tell others "no" or are unable to help; it is a passive-aggressive behavior.

Khalid concurred with Abu Ahmed and added, "My recent experience has shown me that we do not find our friends in the dark days of our life."

I said, "Asking a friend for some assistance is like a litmus test that measures the reliability of friendship. Most of them may fail the test. What are we suppose to do when we are faced with such circumstances?"

Abu Ahmed replied, "Just accept the fact of life that there are just a few people (and you can count them on your fingers) who rush to help if you need them. Furthermore, ask God that you would like to be able to rely on yourself and will not need anyone's help."

Khalid said, "That is impossible. We have to live in a society and, naturally, we need each other."

✢   ✢   ✢

Another weekly discussion was held in January of 2009. Khalid jumped to a totally different topic. That was the way our discussions went; there was no specific theme that we stuck to.

He began, "I had a serious case of constipation last week, and I have suffered a lot. I was also reading about bowel movements, and it seems that the healthy individual must be like a baby who goes to the bathroom after every meal. Nevertheless, a great percentage of people do not know that a daily bowel movement is a prerequisite to good health and vitality. If you keep the waste inside of you and do not vacate it, it can poison your body and can produce all sorts of health problems. Thus, we have to have at least a couple of bowel movements a day."

"How can we maintain a smooth bowel movement?" asked Abu Ahmed.

Khalid explained, "Through drinking lots of water and eating fruits and vegetables daily."

Then I added, "We also need to train our body to go to the bathroom twice a day even if we do not have anything to get rid of, just to keep the system of our body running. Needless to say, Sigmund Freud has talked about people who tend to be constipated a lot and calls these people an anal personality or an anally retentive individual who tends to be stingy or frugal with their possessions as well as with their emotions. Thus, it is imperative that we train our mind and body to have regular bowel movements and never pass a day without one. Of course, once you have one, there will be a big smile on your face, and that can be very refreshing."

✢   ✢   ✢

Then, during one of our winter evening discussions, Abu Ahmed and Khalid said, "Talib, we always hear that this person is intelligent one, and another person is the stupid one. We would like to hear your thoughts about this since you are a psychologist."

I said, "That is a very complicated one. Of course, there are many intelligence tests in our field that we give to people to measure their intelligence. For example, the "Wechsler Intelligence Scale" is one of them, and there are many other tests. But, my own definition of the intelligent person is different. I learned it from a guru in India. I believe the intelligent one is one who is able to make him/her happy and accept the challenges in life as well as having some problem-solving skills. That is my perspective on intelligence. For example, what is the point if the person has a high intelligence, has published hundreds of books, has acquired huge wealth, or has a great profession, but he or she is a miserable human being or merely an unhappy person? So, the challenge to us is to use our intelligence capability to make ourselves happy individuals."

Then Khalid asked, "And who is the stupid person?"

I replied, "The unhappy one, the one who is unable to enjoy his/her life, or the one who lacks the skills to solve his/her problems or face the challenges that we all have to face once in a while."

Khalid said, "Talib, from this definition, can we conclude that the majority of people are not intelligent?"

"Yes," I said, "and, moreover, the sad fact of reality is that these people are unaware that they are stupid because of their self-deception that happiness is difficult to reach or an illusion as some of the gloomy writers profess."

During one of the summer evenings of 2008, Abu Ahmed said that he had read a book on eastern philosophy and found the following statement: "Never assume importance and you will never lose it."

I responded to his statement. "In our life we tend to attach importance or value to certain things which can be valueless, mainly our attachment to our ego and the assumption that we are important people. Or, we may assume that there are many things in life that are very important and if we lost them, it might bring some pain and suffering. On the other hand, if we assume nothing is important in our temporary life, we can free ourselves from such an awful burden."

"Which means that nothing in this life of ours is important" Khalid asked.

I said, "Yes, to a certain degree."

He then asked, "What about our family and friends?"

I said, "All these people are important in our lives. However, we are talking here about possessions, or position in life, or our profession--but mainly our ego. The assumption of importance for many things in our lives can become cumbersome for us. For example, we spend inordinate amounts of time and energy defending the importance of our ego; consequently, we are drained and tired. Thus, if we never have such assumptions, our lives are lighter and freer."

❖　❖　❖

During one of the last year's discussion, Abu Ahmed said, "Listen, Folks. What do you think of complements? I have been receiving a lot of complements lately."

We agreed that it was good, as long as it does not shape us. He asked, "What does that mean?"

Khalid replied, "When people give you a complement, they want you to act or behave accordingly, so there is a subtle manipulation to giving complements. We must be aware of it. However, there is old wisdom that goes like this, 'Be independent of the good or bad judgment of others.'"

This is very profound wisdom. If people judge us as bad or good, it is the same: you have to live with yourself and accept that you have beauty and rubbish inside of you. So, do not be deceived or manipulated by the complement from others. Perhaps it may feed some of our hungry ego. Or, sometime we might do things just to fish for complements or seek recognition.

Then Abu Ahmed said, "Listen, Friends. The human self is a very complicated one."

I said, "Of course. Thus, we need to understand the intricate parts of it."

Khalid said, "So, if someone complements you, you can either take it with a grain of salt or perhaps, they meant well in their complement. And that would be a rarity as far as human motives are concerned."

⁑ ⁑ ⁑

One week in April, 2009, Khalid said that he had heard there was a course on the art of living. "What does that mean?"

We said, "Yes, it is true that living is an art. It is like learning music, or painting a picture, or learning any other art form. However, the majority of us are completely ignorant of such an art because when we came into the world, we were just thrown into the river of life without knowing how to swim.

Then Abu Ahmed asked, "What are the components of the art of living course?"

In response, I provided the following. "The first component is to live in the here and now."

"What does that mean?" they asked.

I continued, "That the past is history and no matter what you do, you will never bring it back or undo what has already been done. It is like when the fall season comes and the tree sheds its leaves. Once the leaves drop from the tree, it is impossible to bring them back to the tree and put life in them again. The past is like a dead leaf; just leave it were it belongs. It can be fertilizer to the ground. As far as the future is concerned, it is in the hands of God, and no one knows what the future holds. And if the past is gone and the future has not yet arrived, what is the point of worrying about either of them? Just try to live your life in the minute of right now and enjoy it because it will go away as well. This is why they call it the 'present' because it is a gift to us. This is the master key component of the art of living."

"The second one is to reduce the chatter of the mind because our mind is like a monkey who jumps from one branch to another. It is cluttered with a lot of thoughts, ideas, judgments, and all sorts of conflicts. Again, we may need to stop the chatter and live in the moment, perhaps just let go, or we take assiduous steps to empty our mind of the chatter. Meditation can be a great tool for that."

"The third component of the art of living course, is that many human beings are not disturbed by the events that happen to them. They are disturbed by their interpretations of the event, or what they tell themselves.

76

Unfortunately, in most instances, our interpretations tend to be negative ones, and we become disturbed by them. Thus, we may need to condition ourselves to see the positive side of each circumstance or event so that we can be a less disturbed people because every event has many probabilities."

Khalid said, "I may add another to the art of living components. You must have a love for God, love for yourself, and love for others. And that can be a great spiritual connection because nothing can fill our empty hearts and keep us serene until we introduce the loving power of God."

Abu Ahmed added, "Not just the heart. Love can also make your mind clear and calm and can bring you inner peace for which all of us yearn."

I said, "Love can be the panacea to our total being."

Our weekly discussions continued until the beginning of fall, 2009. Then I had to leave Abu Dhabi to go to Saudi Arabia, but we kept our friendship kindled by meeting once or twice a year in Morocco since the three of us are infinitely fascinated by Morocco. Undoubtedly, our discussions in Morocco tend to take different colors, those that focus on our intoxication with joyful living in such a happy place.

THE MEANING OF OUR LIFE

I have been struggling for many years about the meaning of our life. Why are we here on the earth? Does God really need us to worship him? Why do most of us live a miserable life? Why do people not know how to be happy? Why do we tend to abuse each other? Why is there so much poverty and illness in the world? Why do people go through serious hardships? Why do we go to war with each other? Or, is our life just a big joke? Maybe we are fooled into believing that our life has meaning, and perhaps it is a meaningless existence. All these questions and inquiries roamed through my mind for many years, and I got depressed over the human condition. Thus, I traveled extensively around the world and have joined many organizations, just to search for the answer to the meaning of our life.

On one of my trips to India 10 years ago, I met a guru in New Delhi, the capital of India, who was close to 90 years of age. I presented him with all these questions. He started to laugh, and then said, "Young man [at that time, I was young enough], life is very simple, but our thinking tends to complicate it. First you must know the basic rules of living. Then, I will give you the meaning of life." In a nutshell, this is what he said.

The First Rule of Living. You must be healthy physically. It is the ultimate priority, which means you must exercise daily, drink a lot of water, eat fruits and vegetables, do not eat dead animals, and fast at least three days a month as well as have an enema once every two months to get rid of the toxicity in your colon.

The Second Rule of Living. You must help others—unconditionally. Try to give without expecting in return. As the old wisdom says, "The only thing that you get to keep is what you give away." Giving can purify the soul. Give more than just materials things, give a smile, be compassionate, help people who are in need of emotional support, be a good listener to your friends and family and give some of your time to be with others.

The Third Rule of Living. Be happy. Everything happens to you for a reason, and normally, the reason is a good reason. Any event that takes place in your life must have a positive interpretation because if you interpret it negatively, you will be frustrated. It is pointless to make a negative interpretation and if you do, you will be the loser. Have faith in the universe that the good will come to you. You may not see it now, but it will come later. God has plans for every one of us. Sometimes we are in a hurry and want the things right now, but God is saying, "Wait, now is not the time." Try to let go of any insult or injury and be forgiving. There is no end to human dysfunction, but be at peace with yourself and with the world around you. Once you have put this formula into action, you will be in true happiness.

Then the guru moved on to the concept of intelligence. He said, "Be intelligent."

And I said, "What does that means?"

He replied, "The intelligent person is not the one who makes good money, or publishes hundreds of books, or reaches a great position in society, or discovers an equation in mathematics. The intelligent person is one who knows how to enjoy life and make him/herself happy. The purpose in life is to be happy, but the sad fact is that the majority of people are miserable beings." Thus, a miserable person is not an intelligent one, but perhaps he is really a stupid one. Then the guru continued his explanation. "Have all the wealth in the world and be what you want to be, but if you are not happy, then you are missing the point of living joyfully."

I felt then that he had defined intelligence from a completely different perspective. "But how can one live life with immense joy?"

The guru explained, "Take these rules and apply them in your personal life, and then you will become happy, healthy, and helpful to others. The meaning in life is an action, not merely a concept. These are the three things that, together, give meaning to your life. He paused. "It is that simple," he exclaimed again.

This conversation between the guru and I lasted over two hours. Afterward, I felt I had discovered a treasure in my life. I felt very light, as if could fly like a bird.

And then, the guru continued. He talked about skills and tools for living. He explained that when we buy a refrigerator, they give us a manual for operating the machine. But, when a human comes to life, we do not have a manual for living. Normally, we come through parents who are illiterate or who do not have a clue as to how to raise a child. In most cases, parents tend to inflict their pathology on their children without even being aware of the damage it might cause. As a result of such an upbringing, we grow up as fearful beings.

Thus, living and raising children require many skills of parents including the ability to provide their children with the tools that enable them to live effectively. Lacking such tools, we may become inadequate human beings. We struggle with many deficits in our life, and not having the appropriate life tools can rip all the joy from our existence.

Living is an art. You can give a person a piano and tell him to play it, but he will never be able to do so until he masters the skills of music. Living requires a lot of skills to enable us to negotiate our emotional side, spiritual side, intellectual side, social side, and so one. If we do not have these skills, we tend to subjugate ourselves to trials and errors in our behaviors. By the time we reach the age of maturity, our life has passed, and it has been wasted.

The guru continued by telling me that growing up a psychologically healthy individual can be a colossal task, one placed either on the parent or on the individual him/herself. Thus, we have to invest in an educational system that first teaches parents how to do their job, and then teaches each of us how to manage our emotions with others and find our own comfortable place in the world. That can be a huge challenge. However, we as a society must pay attention to this so that we can reduce the levels of depression, envy, jealousy, frustration, anxiety, and even hostility towards each other. Perhaps, the guru and I were dreaming of the world of Utopia.

Finally, as our conversation was coming to an end, I held the hand of the guru, kissed it, and wanted to say good-bye to him. He said, "Listen carefully. Try to share these principles and thoughts with all the people that you meet in your life so we can have the dialogue of peace within ourselves as well as with the world that we live in.

I started to apply these principles in my personal life, and it has made a sharp difference in my perspective towards the world. Still, it was not enough for my personal satisfaction or for my restless soul. I felt there must be something else in life beyond these rules, something more meaningful.

I was an atheist most of my life. Fortunately, in 2004 I went through a dramatic spiritual transformation and, as a result, I have developed a strong faith in and love for God. Since then I feel that to derive a meaning for our existence, we must have the love of God in the recesses of our heart. Once we have such a love, then there are no worries or fears in our heart. That love can be translated into a love of self and, consequently, a love of others. That can be very nourishing to the human soul. As they say, love is the answer to all human conditions.

The Psychology of the
Desert Inhabitants

There is much scientific research indicating a serious, profound impact of nature or surroundings on human behavior. Ben Khaldoun, an Arab scholar, wrote thoroughly about this subject in his book, *Introduction*. Human beings interact with nature every single minute of their lives. Thus, nature can shape an individual's characteristics. For example, if nature or the environment is generous (e.g., it has an abundance of water and trees), then those who live in such surroundings may become giving beings. If nature or the environment has a lot of rain and trees, it can have a positive impact on a person. If nature is a desert and has nothing to give except sand and rocks, it may make people less giving, or they can be harsh and less generous because they reflect what nature offers them.

If we observe the inhabitants of our planet, Earth, we can clearly see the influence geography has on human beings. For example, people who live close to the water tend to be more relaxed than people who live in the desert. Or, people who live in very lush, green surroundings tend to be accommodating individuals, while those who live in the desert are less accommodating and self-absorbed. This can explain why Arabs are not a relaxed people. They tend to be agitated and self-centered because they have been living for thousands of years in a harsh desert among sand, rocks, and dry wind. Moreover, the desert has limited resources, and it is stingy and hostile toward its inhabitants. Even though in modern times Arabs have accumulated great wealth, the image of the scarcity of the desert haunts them. And, the poverty of the environment has translated to poverty in their thinking. As a result, the environment has shaped the psychology of people.

The punishment of the desert has a profound impact on the personality of the Arab individual and has imbued them with certain characteristics. For example, they tend to be difficult to deal with, suspicious of others, and greedy because living in the desert is very difficult; they have no control over shifting sand or availability of water. We, as human beings, tend to inherit certain traits in our personalities. The subjugation of living in a harsh environment, one that shows no mercy, for many centuries can make us a hostile people. Similarly, Eskimos who live in a land that has been covered with ice for thousands of years tend to be difficult people. Such a lifestyle may prevent individuals from becoming innovative people.

According to Abraham Maslow's hierarchy of needs, people must first satisfy their basic needs such as the need for food, water, and shelter. Then they can move to the second level of need fulfillment, the need for safety and security.

The Arabs have lived for thousands of years in an empty desert, struggling to meet their basic survival needs: the need for food, water, and shelter--although, the tent has not protected them from the dusty wind. This, then, is sufficient reason for their anxiety over what the next day might bring them.

People often suffer from hunger and thirst and act accordingly. Arabs have not felt safe and secure in the desert since tribes often attacked one another and took the water or the camel from each other to satisfy their hunger or thirst. Therefore, attacking each other was a matter of survival, and taking another's livestock was a normal way to survive.

The third level of need fulfillment is the need to be loved. As human beings we need to feel the sense of warmth being loved provides. Arabs, unfortunately, have not reached this third stage in the hierarchy of need fulfillment. They have continued to struggle with the first and second stages: having food and shelter and having their families and themselves secure from harmful attack.

As a result of the sever influence the desert has on the Arab personality, we can clearly see how certain characteristics developed. For example, Arabs generally lack freedom of expression as well as a sense of wholeness in either themselves or each other.

A basic concept in the science of human behavior tells us that people who struggle with their survival needs tend to have difficulty achieving self-actualization or spiritual connections with other human beings. Even though Arabs are now living a modern lifestyle, the accumulation of thousands of years of hardship remains in their collective consciousness. This is the archetype of which Carl Jung talks, that which we inherit from our ancestors.

Moreover, life in the desert deprives the Arab of living creatively or realizing their personal potential. The focus has been on the self and on what could be acquired for day-to-day survival. Thus, the selfish nature of the Bedouin is the operating norm of the Arab's daily life. The nomadic Arab tribes are always moving to follow the water for grazing and for their survival. As a result, they have not developed an attachment to a piece of land or a country, or in other words, there is no loyalty for their country, and their daily behavior is the best proof of that. Their own personal gain is the primary motive for their behavior, with a resulting serious disregard for the well-being or the welfare of others. These are common attitudes of the Arab's daily lifestyle, and that was why God sent the Prophet Mohammad (peace upon him) to cultivate the cruel nature of the Arab. But, it seems the beautiful teaching of Islam has not changed them fundamentally.

Nature surrounding the Arab is static and is the same in whatever direction they turn their face. This may produce boredom within the individual. On the contrary, people who live in season changing surroundings tend to experience pleasurable meaning in their lives; there is no consistent routine in their life as there is in the desert life. The abundances of water tend to produce a soothing effect upon people, evoking a sense of renewal of life and strength. The best example of such an effect occurs in the city of Curitiba, Brazil, of which 75% is green. According to an environmental report, the inhabitants of the city are very positive people, and the city is considered to be the best place in the world to live.

Sadly enough, the Arab are pouring a lot of concrete and cements in their city as insecure reaction to the Tent life-style which they have lived for thousands of years. Thus, it is imperative that they invest their wealth in making their land green. Nevertheless, the painful fact remains, even now, the Arab are haunted by an inherent psychological insecurity. We have to look for the applicable solution to the predicament that face the Arab and understand how their collective conscious mind works. The new generation of Arabs might remove some of the residues of the long-lasting effects of the desert lifestyle. In the meantime, they must transcend over their hostile situation, and free their souls from the punishment of their environment.

THE PSYCHOLOGY OF RELIGIONS

Mankind has been living on the earth for an eon of time and innately likes to worship anything that they consider to have power over their survival. For example, they have worshipped the stars, moon, sun, thunder, animals, and rocks and they have even made a god out of stone and worshipped it. Mankind has a strong desire to control things around them and they try to assign a power to the things that they cannot control so that they can feel safe. Humans have been very insecure since they descended from Heaven and found out that the earth is a scary and hostile place in which to live. This is why humans are in a constant search for something beyond the self to worship or to find meaning for their existence. Moreover, the fear of death has also been a major force in making humans insecure, and it tends to get worse when they are faced with draught, thunder, earthquake, or even animal attacks. It is an essential part of the human psychology to seek God, the power beyond oneself, when we are weak or faced with danger and undoubtedly we go to God to alleviate some of our anxiety and fear. But, humans are not rational when it comes to seeking a power outside of themselves . They have sculpted a piece of stone, designated a magical power to it, and then they put it in their home to worship, and this practice continues to the present day.

The Almighty God noticed man's strong desire and struggle to worship something, so God sent prophets to deliver messages to the people to guide them through the spiritual darkness in which they live. Of course, each prophet came with a book and a clear message that he delivered to a specific people. For example, Moses (peace upon him) came with the message of Judaism, Jesus (peace upon him) came with Christianity, and the Prophet Mohammad (peace upon him) came with Islam. Although, there were thousands and thousands of prophets who came with different messages, no doubt God sent them to specific troubled spots in the universe. Perhaps, we remember the one who came in recent history. Each prophet brought a message that completed or was a continuation of the pervious one. Prophet Mohammad (peace upon him) came to the Arabs because they were living in total ignorance and spiritual darkness.

The message from God is very clear and loud that you, the inhabitants of the earth, must try to be peaceful, helpful and live in harmony and in loving relationships with each other. That was the predominant message throughout the history of religions. Undoubtedly, human beings took these entire messages and put their own spin on them, and most of the time they twisted the original message from God and structured it according to his own malicious desires and wishes. For example, in the mid-1800s, the Church of Europe issued a decree that buying and selling black people as slaves was allowed in the Christian view. There are numerous examples that we observe these days regarding the killing of a lot of innocent people in the name of religion. Mankind has written his own scriptures to suit his own personal benefit. God kept sending messengers to warn people that if they did not obey the instructions of God, God would punish them. The sad reality is that mankind never listened to the warnings, but defied the order of God.

For example, when Noah was sent by God to his people, asking them to be kind and just to each other, they laughed at him and never believed him. Then God instructed him to build the Ark, and Noah asked the people over and over to obey God, and if they did not obey the order of God, the earth would be flooded and again, they did not listen. Then God began to flood the earth, even Noah's own son did not believe him. He saw the rain coming and the earth beginning to flood. His father, Noah, asked him to get into the ark, but he said, "No, I will go to the mountain and save myself."

Noah said, "Son, I am a prophet, and God will not stop the rain, and it will cover the mountain top and the whole earth. Why do you want to lose your life? Please, son, get in the ship."

His son said, "No, I do not want to get in," and disappointed his father, and then drowned.

It seems that the irrational and the defiant nature of mankind are imbedded in his psyche. God, with great mercy, warns man that this life is a temporary one and it is a mere rehearsal for the eternal one, so man must be patient and pass the test so that they can live forever next to God. But, painfully speaking, the nature of man is impatient and wants immediate gratification over the long-term fulfillment. God has decided "Enough of that" and closed the chapter of sending prophets, saying to man, "I will meet you at the point of no return, the Judgment Day."

Oftentimes, religion becomes a source of serious conflict, and it has been associated with some of the most horrific crimes committed on the face of the earth. There has been a lot of blood shed in the name of religion. People are so dogmatic when it comes to religion. One person may say, "I know the way," and force his way upon others. And, if others do not follow his way, then he may kill them to save them from Hell. Perhaps, we have become totally blind and have no regard for human values. It is the saddest reality of the human condition that these days religion has became a tool for revenge, for abuse, and for ultimate cruelty. Of course, the teaching of religion is very far from all of that, but when human malevolent intent prevails, then the ugly face of humanity appears.

If we look closely at any religion, we may find that it consists of three pillars: faith, conduct and rituals. All these components are clearly spelled out in the books of God. For example, the faith component is the cornerstone of religious belief. The second one mentioned is conduct, or the behavioral component, and it is how people carry and manage themselves in the world around them. Finally, the third component is that of rituals that seems the most prevalent one in religions. Let us take a close look at each one of the components.

The First Pillar is Faith

This pillar is the one that believes that God is the Almighty power, the omnipresence, the omnipotent, the creator of all living and non-living things. Once you have that in the deep recess of your heart, you have the connection to the ultimate loving power which encompasses the whole universe. Having a deep faith can give you the spiritual nourishment that sustains every aspect of your life. Faith is the springboard of everything in one's life. Faith can penetrate your whole being and shine internally as well as radiate outside of you.

Of course, people may pay lip service to faith, but deep down do not have it because they are confusing faith with the practicing of rituals. Faith can swell your heart with love for God, yourself, and the people around you and that can be the utmost solution to human suffering. Faith does not know fear at all because love and fear cannot be in the same heart at the same time. This is a very delicate psychological fact that must be understood: the opposite of love is not hate, it is fear. Having a true faith can make you a sensitive, caring, considerate, and loving human being.

The Second Pillar is Conduct

Conduct, or behavior, is the second pillar. As they say, "Please do not tell me or preach to me, just show me." Your behavior reflects your religious belief as displayed in your attitude and conduct. The teachings of religion are manifested in a one's behavior toward their fellow humans, the carrying of oneself in such a manner that is in accordance with the welfare of fellow humans. Diabolically, our behavior can be the opposite of what we profess. This is why we see people who are cynical when it comes to religion. We have lost faith in religious people who always shout so loud while their actions do not match their rhetoric. This is called hypocrisy.

The Third Pillar is Ritual

Unfortunately, ritual is the most dominant of all religious practices. You may see people spend inordinate amounts of time and energy just practicing any kind of ritual that can oftentimes be empty of any spiritual fulfillment. Practicing rituals is merely a habit that people may have learned in their early childhood; they grew up with such rituals. These practices have exceeded all other pillars of religion and are not confined to one religion; it is so with all religions. Perhaps, the times spent in the practice of rituals are immense and can be at the expense of the pillars of faith or conduct.

Why it is that faith requires a fundamental challenge to the core of our soul, while the practice of rituals can be an empty one that we observe in our parents or the people around us and we follow them? The practice of rituals can serve deep psychological purposes. It may give us certain false satisfaction that we are connected to God (even though our heart is void of faith). Or, we may like to be seen by others, perhaps just showing off. Or, it may give us certain power, or we may use it to manipulate or gain an advantage over others through certain practices. Faith, on the other hand, is mainly a relationship only between an individual and God, and no one else knows about it.

Conclusion

Humankind is yearning for a psychological union with the creator since we were separated when Adam committed the defiant act, and God ordered him to leave Paradise. We are frantically seeking to be reunited with the omnipotent. We are wandering aimlessly on the earth, and we have created many gods just to sooth our pain of separation.

All of humanity prays daily to alleviate suffering. While, some suffering is self-inflicted, others are inflicted by fellow humans. In addition, there is suffering that has been inflicted upon us by nature (natural disasters) when God gets angry with us. Furthermore, when humans are unhappy within themselves, they tend to lash out at the people around them. Human have not been happy for a while, thus, they tend to wage wars with his fellow humans in the name of religion or nationality or for whatever reason he might invent. Perhaps, the greatest enemy to humans is themselves, because we are born with irrational, destructive tendencies. Here, we specifically mean the male gender because the female gender differs in their perspective. The female does not like war, they want to protect their own offspring, and they see blood in their monthly menstruation. The male, on the other hand, wants to see blood in war. Perhaps, religious teachings try to put a cap on this tendency.

Another observation is that religions collectively have corrected some of the human nature. However, the focus of religion is on practicing rituals that can be simply a performance of any mechanical act, and it can be void of any meaning that could bring true change to the heart of man. The heart of man is still filled with fear, anxiety, worry, and greed because the focus is not on pure faith. This is why we see the majority of the populations of the world suffering from a shortage of food, diseases, and, most of all, depression. The ultimate solution for the human dilemmas as far as religion is concerned is to cultivate our heart and soul with true faith and love of God, allowing us to be happy and to share what we have with our fellow humans.

KINDRED SPIRIT

Bali is an island located on the south part of Indonesia. It is one of the most beautiful places on the earth—lush and green with lots of wildflowers. The fruits and vegetables are very delicious, and it has one of the cleanest beaches in the world with white sand and relaxing ocean waves. The people are very kind and humble. Bali is the only Buddhist place in Indonesia; the rest is Muslim. The people have many traditions related to fire, and they have a wonderful fire ceremony.

In 1986, I visited the island and rented a place right on the beach. Normally, people ride a motorcycle to travel to Denpasar, the capital of Bali. The capital is a crowded place, and peddlers are everywhere, each one doing their own thing. I walked through a poor section of the town, which is what I do when I travel so I can discover the real people of the country. The section had narrow streets, and you could find sheep and cows roaming the streets with people. Women were sitting in front of their houses, either weaving or knitting clothes for their families.

I was carrying my camera and wandering in that part of Denpasar when suddenly, I was faced by a woman who was sitting in front of her house knitting a cloth. I looked at her, and she looked back at me, and there was a moment of silence between us. I did not say anything to her, but I felt electrified and went into a trance for a minute or so and almost lost my sense of time. Then I walked away and continued my foot exploration of the town.

I was walking and did not understand what had just happened to me regarding the woman. I kept thinking about her and that whole scene in my mind--the way she looked at me, and the way she was knitting the cloth. My mind was busy trying to recapture what had just happened to me. At the end of the day I went back to the beach home which I had rented and sat on the beach looking at the blue water of the ocean, just thinking about that woman. It was evening time and when the night came, I retreated to my room and lay down on my bed, the image of that woman still in my mind. I started to blame myself, wondering why in the world had I not talked to her or even said hello to her. Was I a cowardly man unable to initiate a word with a stranger? Normally, I am not a shy person and, without hesitation, always initiate a conversation with a stranger throughout my travels around the world.

But in this instance, some sort of paralysis took place within me, and I was unable to say anything to her. I spent that night just thinking about her and how to find her again even though the chances of finding her were very slim. Then, sleep overtook me.

I woke up the next day with a feeling of hope that I would find her. I had my breakfast and then took a motorcycle to Denpasar at the same time of day that I had seen her before, close to noontime. Now I had to find my way to her place or to the section of town where I walked the day before. I started to walk in a different part of the town, and I felt I may have lost my way to her place. Here, I started to squeeze my brain to remember the part of town where I had walked the day before. I was even thinking about an extraordinary power to help me to find her place, and I prayed that my confusion would clear up and would find her place.

All of the sudden, I found myself at her place, looking at her. She was sitting in front of her home weaving a cloth. I looked at her, and she smiled back with such anticipation. I went to her and said hello. She answered me in her native language, Bahasa, the language of Indonesia, but I heard her saying, "Hello, Talib."

I was stunned on hearing my name, but, I thought that maybe I was just delusional at the time, that it was just in my mind. How did she know my name when I had never even talked to her before? I said to her, "I would like to invite you for lunch or dinner."

She said, "Just give me a half an hour to put myself together and wait for me."

I just kept walking in the area to pass the time while she dressed up and came out to me. Right away, without any reservation, I held her hand, and she did the same, as if we had known each other for many years. We walked towards the bus station to go to the beach home where I lived.

I introduced myself, and she said, "I know your name is Talib."

I was flabbergasted! "How do you know my name?"

She replied, "I will tell you later, and my name is Freda."

We went to a restaurant to have some food, and it was close to the evening time. Then, we went to the beach, and we both sat to watch the sunset there. Of course, she and I never left each other's sight, and we held hands all the time. There was an instant and intense connection between us. I felt there was a mystery about this woman that needed to be explored.

Freda was well over the age of 30 years, and the color of her skin was an earthy color which I considered the color that God gave it to his favorite people. Sometimes this color is called wheatish in India, or sometimes it is called bronze or Mulatto in Brazil or call Kayumanggi color in Philippine, and it is called brownish in this part of the world. It has many names, but it happens to be the color that has always fascinated beauty lovers, and it is the color of my beloved mother.

We talked a lot, and I felt I was facing an extraordinary situation. I did not understand the Bahasa language, nor did Freda understand the English language. How did we communicate? I have no clue. We really got into very deep conversations, like politics, world affairs, sex, human relationships, and so on. After that, we went to the local bar to have a drink and then, close to midnight, we went to my beach home. We continued our deep discussion; then we made love to each other. It was soul connection experience. The immensity and the depth of love left me elated. I felt we both reached the Peak Experience [as was described by Carol Rogers]. She lifted up my soul to the state of Nirvana, the highest state of happiness according to the Buddha religion.

Freda was a woman who gave her total self in love making. I felt the same, and she wanted to be part of my total being. When she kissed me, my whole body shivered. Her orgasm lasted all night long, and she invigorated me sexually .I did not know where all that energy came to her to last that long. The spiritual connection between us was so profound that we felt as if we were one person. There was a merging between us at many levels--emotional, spiritual, and physical, as well as the soul level.

I felt that Freda's spirit was the one who communicated with me, not her tongue. That is why we understood each other so well, even though we did not speak the language of each other. This was very puzzling to me, but not to her. It seems that Freda knew about this encounter beforehand, but there was something between us that I found hard to explain.

The talks between us never stopped, and I realized that this experience was not usual. But, I felt I should not insert my disturbing thoughts into it though normally, this is what I did. I said to myself, "Just flow with it and enjoy the moment."

The morning came, and we took our breakfast, and then went to the sea to swim together. Freda was a great swimmer, and we started to play in the water and laugh a lot like a children. We both felt incredible joy derived from being together. When it was noon time, Freda took me to the room, and we indulged ourselves in fabulous sex. Freda was a master at lovemaking and a very intelligent woman in the relationship. She let me feel wanted, loved, adored, appreciated, and most of all, she conveyed to me that I was the only man in her life. And, perhaps, that rarely happens for any man. Once you feel that you are the one and only by woman, you are the most fortunate man in the world. And I was the most fortunate man at that moment. Freda was so passionate about me, and she tantalized every minute of our time with affection and love.

Freda stayed with me another day, and the time we spent together was just a gift to each other, and every minute of the time was so precious. We talked about our personal lives; what made us happy, what made us sad, about our dreams, and so on.

On the third day, Freda asked me to marry her, but, as an insecure person about the responsibility of marriage, I said "no." referring to the stupid cliché that I learned in the West, "that we do not know each other." And, we did not know the language.

She said, "Talib, we have been doing fine and communicating very well with each other. Please do not say 'no.'" Then, with such a strong tone in her voice, she said, "Talib, now you need to listen carefully to understand our story and how I came to know your name in the first place. I will tell the whole story."

Freda continued. "When I saw you the first time, and you looked at me, and you did not talk, that look infiltrated my deep soul, and I felt an overwhelming instant attraction towards you. I was so disturbed that day, and wondering how I could find you again. I could not concentrate on anything and just felt lost. There was a wise and spiritual counselor woman, a neighbor to me, who knows how to uncover human hidden thoughts. I talked to her about you. She told me, 'He is from a distant land, and his name is Talib, and he is your soul mate.' She suggested to me that I should stay close to my home because you would come back to look for me. And she even gave me the approximate time when you would come back to look for me, which was 2:00 in the afternoon. She also told me that I would have a serious spiritual connection with you. Perhaps it would last, but probably it would not last, but that I should try to make it last because you are the missing part in this world. And that our spirits are kindred to each other."

Freda explained that this was how she came to know my name. "Please, Talib, this is a lifetime opportunity. Try not to lose it, and let us be together."

I said, "Freda, I am not good material for marriage."

She replied, "I will make you wonderful material for marriage."

By the end of the third day, I took Freda back to her home in Denpasar and kissed her goodbye. She was deeply saddened, and then she turned her face to me and said, "Talib this is the last chance for you in your lifetime, and if you do not take it, you will regret it--not now, not tomorrow, not next year, but you will regret it for the rest of your life. Please, do not be stupid and lose such a gift that the universe has presented to you."

But, I said, "no," with a lot of pain and confusion. Then I left her and since that time until now, I truly regretted it.

I went back to my beloved hometown, Detroit, Michigan, and slid into severe depression. I was calling Freda once in a while. Her family forced Freda to marry her cousin, an illiterate farmer. She gave birth to one boy and one girl; she named the boy Talib and the girl Sara. She sent me a picture of her son, and his features are similar to mine. I kept minimum contact with her because she was a married woman. Then the family moved completely to central Java, Indonesia, and I lost any contact with her.

Life has presented me with a wonderful gift, but fear played a major factor in preventing me from developing my relationship with Freda. And, perhaps, the garbage in my mind that I might find someone better than her may have also contributed to that.

The disturbing fact about our behavior as human beings is that we do not value or cherish what we have and would rather look to what we do not have. We have conditioned our minds about certain things when it comes to relationships. It is like a real estate list. For example, when you want to buy a home, you have a list of specifications in your mind for the home, and you keep looking until you find that home. We so often deal with human beings like real estate specifications, and when an opportunity presents itself, we may overlook it or just take it for granted. Then years pass, and we may look back and say, "Oh, I wish that I had seized that opportunity". We as an educated people often like to complicate life because we live life through the rubbish of our analytical thinking.

INGREDIENTS FOR HAPPINESS

First of all, let us define happiness; it is the state of joy, contentment, gladness, and pleasure or felicitous. It is the most important state of being. Our purpose of living is to be happy, and we should never compromise this purpose by any means, otherwise, we are defeating the purpose of our existence. However, there are many questions that need to be answered in this journey. For example: Why are the majority of the people unhappy? Is there any relationship between wealth and happiness? Are there any secret ingredients to our happiness? What are the stumbling blocks that stand in the way of happiness? Are there any skills that need to be learned to master our happiness? Initially, we will try to identify the stumbling blocks to our happiness, and then we will spell out the ingredients for happiness.

The question oftentimes asked is "Why aren't people happy". No doubt, it depends on individual cases as well as their circumstances. There are some people who are born with a certain tendency to be unhappy because of their genetic make-up. According to the International Conference in Mental Health held in Greece in August, 2009, one of the clear observations in our recent times is that the number of depressed people around the world is increasing. That the number of people who are depressed exceeds the number of people who suffer from heart attacks or other major illnesses is a serious challenge facing the human community. It seems the population of our planet, Earth, is becoming more depressed than happy.

According to a concept presented by many behavior scientists, including

Erich Fromm in his book, *To Have or To Be*, as long as we are in the mode of "having," there will be no happiness; we need to shift to the mode of "being." What does that mean? We are not aware of ourselves, and we are accepting a lies from others who tell us that we have to have material goods and more money so we can be happy. We spend a great portion of our lives accumulating things, either wealth or materials possessions or position. Once we have arrived and have gained what we have been busy with, we are faced with a bitter fact of life, which life is empty after acquiring all that we have. It is like a mirage. We are conditioned to crave such things because our personal values are associated with how much we have, rather than with our being.

Where is the fault here? Of course, the entire society, our educational system, and all our institutions have indoctrinated us that in having lies the ultimate happiness. In other words, we are flirting with our primitive greed tendency. Moreover, our greed tendency is bottomless, and there is no satiation to it. It is like a black hole in the atmosphere which sucks in everything that comes its way. Our greed urge tends to force us to do anything just to have. Consequently, our life is wasted in a constant effort of having, and by the time we realize that, it is too late to do anything because the cancerous tumor of having has mastitis. Greed is the new form of disease that has infected humanity. People are running just to have more and more. And at the end, they sense the emptiness, the shallowness, and the dissatisfaction with their material possessions.

Numerous psychological studies clearly indicate that rich people are slightly happier than poor people. And also they feel insecure and have more worries because they feel that they may lose their wealth. Nevertheless, the mode to have stems from our personal insecurity. Thus, we have to shift our perception to contentment with what we have, and to be satisfied.

Sadly enough, we are living in an impoverished environment as far as happiness is concerned. Hence, another reason for our unhappiness is that we, as human beings, have a strong desire to be miserable beings. It is no surprise that a psychoanalytic school of thought by Sigmund Freud has unearthed that human beings can find pleasure in their misery, the "pleasure in pain principle." Of course, that can be very difficult to treat unless we go deep into the recesses of our unconscious mind and uncover such hidden desires.

Another contribution to not being happy is that we have been told that life is a painful journey, and happiness is a myth. This message has been ingrained in our minds for a long time by many of the people around us, but has been mainly accentuated by the people in eastern cultures. Thus, we think happiness is something very far away, at a remote distance, and hard or impossible to attain. This is why wherever you look, you see people who are in a general state of malaise. No doubt, there might also be many difficult circumstances that surround some people that may contribute to their unhappiness. But, what we need is either to change those circumstances, or to accept what is unchangeable, and to know the difference as they say in AA meetings. So, a closer look at the contributing factors of unhappiness has provided us with the reasons why we are not a happy people.

Now, what are the ingredients that you must have to cook the delicious dish of happiness? The number one ingredient of this recipe is awareness; you must be aware that you are an unhappy person because there are numerous people who have no clue that they are unhappy. Once you become aware of your state, then you must identify the sources of your unhappiness. Secondly, you must make a personal commitment to do what it takes to make yourself happy. Unfortunately, some people unconsciously feel that they do not deserve to be happy.

Being happy does not come naturally; it is a skill, a form of art or science that you have to master. It is like the art of painting a picture, or playing music, or writing a poem--you have to dedicate time to hone such skills so that you are able to do it. The art of happiness is more sophisticated than any art form. It is also said that being happy is more difficult than being depressed. Thus, you need to know practically and precisely what to do in order to obtain such a stage of happiness. The following steps summarize the ingredients of happiness.

1. Being healthy physically is the bedrock of happiness. You must have a healthy body as well as a healthy mind. Free yourself from illness by leading a balanced life and watching what you eat. This may not come easily or you might just be lazy; you have to work hard at it with a concrete knowledge of

the basic roles of good health. Try to understand how the body functions, and set up your frame of mind in wellness.

2. Try to live according to your own wishes, not the wishes of others. In other words, just be the way you are and try not to please others at the expense of your own self. Do not say "yes" when you want to say "no." Be assertive in what you want in the space of your life, and that can free you from internal conflict.

3. Find a job, or an occupation, or a business that you like to do to support yourself financially and that, perhaps, is meaningful enough to derive some joy from what you do.

4. Try to surround yourself with a circle of positive friends who try to bring out the best in you, and run away from people who try to bring out the worst in you, even if they are family members.

5. Find yourself a supportive, encouraging, uplifting partner in life. This part is an indispensable one, with no compromises at this level. Moreover, do not live the life of mediocrity with your partner. Try to live a loving, harmonious life with your partner. Sexual fulfillment is the antidote of a happy partnership. Perhaps you may ask what the parameter of fantastic sex is. The answer is that when the two of you finish love making, and there is a smile on each of your faces and you want to have more. No doubt, boredom can creep into the relationship, but try to be creative to bring some electricity to it. Sex is a very essential part of communication; it is the backbone that sustains a relationship. Needless to say, the majority of us do not have such a partner, or perhaps some of us get lucky. Or, we may need to be satisfied with what we have because the nature of life does not give you what you want, there is always something missing in one's life.

6. You must have a strong spiritual bond with the ultimate loving power of the universe. You may call it God, or whatever you call it; just derive spiritual nourishment from this relationship because it is the food for the soul. Otherwise, life without such a bond can be empty and void.

7. Involve yourself in a hobby that you like to practice in your free time, once you have such hobby then boredom may does not touch you.

8. Physical exercise is imperative in the recipe for happiness. Try to engage in physical exercise on a regular basis because it increases your

endorphins in your brain and gives you a sense of wellbeing. Exercise can be also a safeguard from any physical illness.

9. Mental challenge is also essential for living a happy life, and it can sharpen your brain. Solomon said, "As the iron sharpens the iron, so man can sharpen the other." To do this, simply try to be involved in reading, writing, or mental debates.

10. Train yourself to look at any situation or event from a positive perspective and try to orient yourself to several interpretations of any circumstance. This can be a very helpful translation in conserving your energy.

11. To be one with the universe is a very essential part of happiness-- oneness with every living thing, human, tree, animal, and so on. Separation can cause serious alienation from the rest of the planet's inhabitants. In other words, consider yourself a caring member of the human community, one who has the welfare of others in his/her heart.

12. The final ingredient is to get out of yourself. In the words of the old wisdom, "In order to find yourself, just get out of yourself," which means egocentricity can stand in your way of happiness. Just remove the Ego, and be a giving person.

Undoubtedly, most behavior scientists agree that a guideline for happiness is essential in training people to change their frame of mind and consider life a journey of joy.

Metaphysical Meaning of Illness

She came to see me for a psychological consultation in 2001 while I was working in Michigan. She said that she was suffering from severe depression as a result of her early stage of breast cancer. She said she lived in California and she was visiting her sister in Michigan for a few weeks. She informed me that she has time for just a few therapeutic sessions. I said, "I will try to design a short-term treatment plan, and we can work together. However, can we look into how you have developed the breast cancer? She said it was a long story, and I said, "I am listening."

Jennifer began.

✤   ✤   ✤

I am 35 years old and grew up in California. I am the younger of two sisters. I grew up in a very insecure and restless home. There was no sense of peace there, even though our financial situation was fine, and we lived in a very prestigious neighborhood. My father is a very angry man, and my mother is a passive-aggressive woman who knows how to instigate trouble and conflict with my father. My father has been working in a shipyard, and my mother was working as a school teacher. Both of them are retired now. They do not like each other at all. They are constantly fighting, and our home was just Hell. That is why my sister and I got married early around 20 years of age, just to get away from the atmosphere of our home. My older sister is married and living in Michigan. I got married and I am living in California.

Needless to say, when we go out as a family to restaurants or movies we tend to maintain the façade that as if we are from a trouble-free home. Even my father often times treats my mother very well outside the home. But inside the home they are abusive and disrespect each other. My sister and I have interfered numerous times when we see the fights take place between them and when we hear very insulting words from both of them. My sister and I have reached the conclusion that our parents love to be abusive toward each other. Maybe, they got used to it, or they did not know a better way to relate to each other, or their self-worth stems from the chaotic life that they have lived. Or, they both had elements of a sadomasochist personality. All these hypotheses may explain the behavior of my parents. It is very difficult to figure out human motives or behavior.

Then one day when I was a teenager about 15 years old, I came home from school and found my parents brutally beating each other. I jumped in the middle to help my mother and then my father pushed me so hard that I fell down on my head and hit the concrete floor, and I lost consciousness. My mother called the ambulance and they came and took me to the hospital. But, neither of them went with me to the hospital because they both had blood all over their clothes and did not want to be embarrassed or seen by the neighbors.

On the way to the hospital while I was in and out of consciousness, the paramedic woman bent over me and sucked on my breast and rubbed my private part with her hand. I woke up in the middle of that, and saw her bending over and kissing me. I had no energy to talk or to say anything. I just wanted to reach the hospital.

I stayed in the hospital overnight and none of my family came to check on my condition, not even my sister. I was a teenager then and was very fearful. I am 35 years old and have three children. I did not know what to do regarding the ambulance incident, so I just kept it to myself and started to hate my breast and felt I was violated in that part of my body.

✢　✢　✢

Jennifer said, "As you can see, I am a woman who is endowed with large breasts. I always stand before the mirror and say, I wish I did not have this breast. I feel disgusted with my breast, and this part of my body I despise. I was recently diagnosed with breast cancer on my left side."

"Is that the one you saw the paramedic sucking" I asked.

She replied, "Yes."

I said, "Listen carefully Jennifer. Since your cancer is in the early stage, it can be prevented from further development. You may need to follow a regimented program that I will design for you. The program will consist of building up the strength of your immune system so you can fight the cancer."

"Just give me time to think about it," she said.

I asked, "Don't you really want to think about healing yourself?"

Then I said, "Take your time."

She came for the next session and said, "Doc, I do not think I want to do the program."

"Tell me, Jennifer, what is on your mind".

She explained, "Since I developed the cancer my husband, my mother, my father and the whole family have started to call me and come to visit me often. I feel the cancer has done wonders for me. It has brought my family closer to me. I am getting a lot of attention and love, and I do not want to lose that, so let it be."

"I respect your opinion," I said, "but illness is no fun and health can be more enjoyable than illness."

"Not for me," she said. "I am becoming very close to my parents which I have always needed that. My husband calls me several times a day from his work and he never did that before. My sister, who always competed with me, now calls on me with her husband."

Jennifer continued, saying, "To sum it up, Doc, I am becoming the center of attention for the whole family. I just love it and want to keep it going. I do not want it to stop by healing myself. Moreover, next week I will be going back to California. I am telling you that this is my last session with you."

I said, "Please keep me posted regarding the stage of the cancer and be well Jennifer.

The analysis of this case is that there is a statement by Hippocrates, the father of western medicine, which says, "If someone wishes for good health, one must first ask oneself if they are ready to do away with the reasons for their illness, only then is it possible to help them."

Jennifer has developed breast cancer as a result of internalizing the hate to that specific part of her body. Our organs are intelligent, and once they feel that you do not like a specific part of your body, the organs start to develop illness. It is like rejecting that part of your body.

There is another case that I have seen in my practice which testifies to the fact that our illness' can be cooked in the back stage of our mind without us being aware of it and then it manifests itself in our body. This case is about an older woman who has five children and all of them have neglected her for many years and they never have visited her or even called her. She started to hate the place where she carried those children, which of course is her uterus. And eventually, she developed cancer in her uterus. Our organs are vulnerable to any suggestion.

Illness never happens arbitrarily. It may start from inside our psychology and then manifests itself in the body. Our body becomes the battleground for unresolved psychological conflicts. We have to be mindful of any inner conflicts because they can surface in the body later on. Subliminal messages that we may tell ourselves can also have a profound impact on our health.

Perhaps, we need to define illness. It is the imbalance in our life physically, psychologically, and mentally. And if there is any imbalance that happens in one of these three dimensions then an illness will surface.

Jennifer was attracting negative attention to her breast by rejecting that part of her body, thus cancer developed. Oftentimes, the most frequent causes of an illness are negative attitudes, unexpressed emotions, guilt feelings, the need for attention and the need to escape an unpleasant situation. Therefore, certainly an illness can serve as a hidden psychological purpose. For example, if you ask anyone, "Do you want to be healthy?" the answer is, "Of course, I want to be healthy." But once you tell someone to try to follow the basic rules of healthy living, then they say, "I cannot do it." It is like everyone wanting to go to Heaven, but no one wants to die. If you want to go to Heaven, you have to die first. If you want to be healthy, there are a set of rules to follow. In Jennifer's case, she wanted attention, and that is why she wants to keep the cancer in her breast. As strange as it may sound, that was the reality of her illness.

In conclusion, the physical body cannot create an illness by itself, but it can be created by the soul, or by the spirit that moves the body, or by the energy of every cell in our body. The cells work in harmony and in accord with each other to function optimally. If one cell acts independently, the whole body will be in total trouble. Cells have memory. For example, in the case of cancer, the cells may lose their memory and grow beyond their surroundings. The Ayurveda medicine of India clearly supports this concept.

Moreover, two elements can play major roles in our illness. One is that an illness that affects a specific part of our body does not happen by mere chance. It occurs because of hidden emotional or psychological imbalance. It may not even be obvious to the person who carries the illness. This is why we have to teach the patient the first principle of healing which is to be aware of one's inner dynamics of illness. The second element is that our negative attitudes towards one part of our body can greatly contribute to our illness. Psychoanalytic thought has unearthed many scenarios when it comes to illness or health that takes place in the recess of our unconscious mind. Louise Hay has written a very thoughtful book called "Heal Yourself". The theme of the book is that our emotional wellbeing may play a very profound role in our healing. Sometimes we may inherent a certain illness and it stays in our body. It can be manifested only when we become weak or vulnerable psychologically, or when we go through a difficult time in our life which may reduce our resistances to illness. At that point the body starts to present us with all sorts of illnesses.

The human being is a very complex creature, and we may use illness as a way of punishing ourselves because of guilt. For example, if there is a suppression of violence or aggression toward the world and we are unable to channel it out, we may direct it inwardly against ourselves and we become ill. I recall a case in which a woman who slapped her mother on the face and she felt so guilty about it that she literally paralyzed the hand with which she had slapped her mother.

Specific personality types tend to associate with certain illnesses. For example, the diabetic individual has no "sweet" in them are a type C personality who keeps things inside and is not an expressive person. People who have heart trouble are not open people, and they lack love in their life. Again, Louise Hay has dealt with many cases in this regard. No doubt, there is a lot of evidence-based medicine which supports the argument regarding personality-based illnesses.

The key to liberating ourselves from illness is to live in harmony and balance, both internally and externally with the world around us. The dynamics of illness even goes back to our childhood and how much attention we have received when we were sick. We may like unconsciously, to replay that feeling of childhood again in our adult life. The other important key to good health is self-worth and the reliance on our internal resources to supply us with self-acceptance, rather than reliance on others' approval. Once you have that, then you unlock the blockages of illness.

HONOR KILLING

I grew up in the city of Babylon, a child playing in the streets with the rest of the children in the neighborhood. We all enjoyed the free time after we finished our school. That was in late 1960. However, when it is rained, we felt much stressed because the streets were muddy and dirty and we had to stay home. Also, our homes did not have the modern conveniences for the entertainment of children so we used to make our own toys. At that time, life was simple, and we were all innocent children. We just took what life gave us with grace.

There was a girl or, should I say, a young lady in our neighborhood by the name of Najat. She was just gorgeous and very kind and all the children liked her very much. She would give us some candies which was always a treat for us. At that time she was perhaps the age of 20 years old. She had a younger sister, but she was not as beautiful or friendly as Najat. She also had one brother who used to play with us. All the people in the neighborhood liked Najat. She was such a delightful person and very humble, and she could talk with any of the people. And, most of all, she was not mean to the children like so many neighbors.

Then one day we heard that Najat got engaged, and she was going to get married soon. We children felt very sad about Najat leaving the neighborhood. After a few weeks, the preparation for the marriage started to take place in the neighborhood, and none of us were happy that Najat, the kindest, most considerate woman, was leaving the neighborhood. A celebration would take place when the groom's family would arrive. It is the tradition that a group of men from the family of the groom come and take the bride. A local musical band played and all the children in the neighborhood were dancing in the streets. Everyone was giving us candies and it was such a joyful occasion. They brought a carriage pulled by a horse to carry Najat. She waved to us to say goodbye because she was leaving to go to her groom's home which was very far from our neighborhood.

All of the children literally felt sad and happy but happy for her on getting married because marriage is a big deal in Iraq, and also sad because such a wonderful woman was leaving the neighborhood. The tears were in our eyes when she looked at us, and she also had tears in her eyes. She said to all of us children, "Do not worry. I will come once in a while to visit my family and will see all of you. We all said goodbye and wished Najat the best of luck. That summer night the carriage pushed its way through the crowd, and Najat went to her new family, the family of her groom.

After a few days we heard people in the neighborhood saying that Najat was coming back, and we, as children, did not understand what that meant. We learned that the groom was sending her back to her family because he found that she was not a virgin woman and that could be pure disaster to her family and even to the neighborhood. We all felt really sad and disappointed. Three days later she came back, and we saw her crying. We wanted to talk to her to say hello, but her father was a very mean man and said, "I do not want any child in front of my house."

We then heard the people in the neighborhood saying that her father was planning to kill her. What we learned later was that when the groom came to her and found her not a virgin, he told her father to come and get his daughter because she was not virgin. The father went and brought Najat home, but, of course her father belonged to a large family and that was a stain on the honor of the whole family.

They asked Najat who she had had sex with, and she said, "I did not have sex with anyone."

They asked why she was not a virgin, and she said, "I was raped by a man who is well known in the neighborhood." And, Najat told them the story. She was a friend of the man's daughter, and one day when she went to his home to visit his daughter, he grabbed her and raped her. She kept it a secret and was afraid to tell anyone, even his daughter or her own family because it could be catastrophic to everyone.

After her father heard Najat's story, he went to the man and asked, "Did you rape my daughter?" He admitted that he had raped her, and that he would marry her.

Again, as part of the culture, if a man has sex with a woman, he must marry her or he could be killed. The next day the man disappeared from the neighborhood, and it was said that he had moved to another city in Iraq. Her father then needed to deal with the shame that Najat had brought to the family, and, as they said, he needed to clean up the shame by killing Najat.

When no one in the neighborhood saw Najat, her mother told everyone that Najat's father was planning to kill her soon to clean up the shame.

Our home had a higher roof than Najat's home and in the summertime, people normally sleep on the roof of their house because it is too hot to sleep inside the house. Early one morning I heard screaming and loud crying. I looked from our roof to Najat's house, and I saw the most painful scene of my entire life. Najat was struggling and begging her father to leave and her father was trying to put a pillow on her face to kill her. That scene lasted for about 20 minutes, Najat was fighting for her life and, eventually, her father put the pillow over her head and sat on her for a few minutes. He was a very large and obese man. When he left, Najat was gasping for breath and then she dropped dead.

I was watching it all and crying, feeling helpless and begging her father to please leave her. But, of course, he did not hear me. I saw other people from neighboring houses watching as well, but they did not say anything. They called the police, and they came to take Najat to the funeral home. I went down crying, but the rest of the neighbors were happy. They said it was good, and they went to congratulate Najat's father because he had cleaned up the honor of the family from the shame by killing his daughter. There was a sense of silence in the neighborhood, and the feelings were mixed. Some felt that they were supposed to kill the man, who had raped her, but he had moved overnight to a different town, and Najat was now the one who had lost her life.

I talked with people and my family about Najat. However, it seemed the people were just used to such tragic scenes. The feeling among them was numbness.

The police arrested Najat's father, and he was sentenced to three years in prison. Her family was left without any financial support because he had been the breadwinner. She had a younger brother who started to work as a porter at the local farmers' market, carrying fruits and vegetables for people. However, that provided a meager living and did not support the family which consisted of Najat's sister, her brother, and her mother.

Her mother wore black clothes which meant that she was mourning her daughter's death. The search for the man who raped Najat continued, and they finally found him. I heard later that he paid her family some money, and they let him go without any punishment.

The father spent two years in prison, and the family visited him once a month. Then he was infected with tuberculoses. At that time, treatment was difficult in the crowded prison, and he died. So, the family lost their daughter and their father. Their lives were sad and unfortunate, and they were very poor people.

The merit of this story is that honor killing still exists in some parts of the Arab world, such as Iraq, Jordan, and some parts of Egypt. With the exception of in the United Arab Emirates where I lived for seven years, I did not hear about any single case of honor killing because they are not as harsh in their treatment of woman.

Why do Arabs kill their women if they find they are not virgins? Because the Arab has placed his honor on the woman's vagina, and if she loses it, the whole culture collapses. This is not an Islamic way because the teachings of Islam clearly indicate that if you accuse a woman of having sex with a man, then you have to bring in four witnesses, while in the case of a killing, Islam requires only two witnesses. Islam is aware of the Arab psychology that requires four witnesses, which makes such an accusation difficult to prove. Islam knows the Arab well, and Prophet Mohamed (peace be upon him) tried very hard to change some of the cultural practices.

Pre—Islamic practices was to bury a young woman alive as a result of fear that she may bring a shame to the family, but Islam has forbid such cruel practice. Virginity is a national obsession in the Arab culture, and if the woman is not a virgin, it means she has put the honor of the family down in the dirt. The father or the brother must kill her so they can have some respect in society. If they do not kill her, the shame will be attached to them for the rest of their lives and they would lose their respect in their community, and no one would marry the woman from this family. Moreover, there are a lot of doctors in Arab countries who are now specializing in restoring virginity to a woman who has lost it. It is such a waste. We need to have a healthy understanding of our sexuality!

The Arabs are not alone in this regard. The European society also has an obsession with sexuality. They used to have chastity belts placed around the woman's private part when her husband went to war, and he would take the key with him. Man has acted unintelligently to control women's sexuality. In one part of southern India, a woman's vagina is considered a sacred organ. Thus, there is a temple in which to worship the vagina. Moreover, if we look at the artwork of mankind, we can see that vagina symbols are everywhere in places of worship. There is a clear fascination with a woman's private part. Perhaps, because we come from the vagina and man feels he has to protect that organ. I have even read a myth from Africa which states that a group of women went to the forest to collect wood for a fire, and they were faced with a lion coming to attack them. They pulled up their clothes and faced the lion with their vagina. The lion freaked out and ran away from them. It seems that seeing the vaginas even scared the lion. Another myth among the Arabs is that if you look at the vagina long enough, your vision becomes weak. Through these myths and other stories, it is clear that people believe the vagina has some mystical quality. All these stories and myths attempt to highlight the value of this part of a woman's body and show how much we are fascinated with it.

Najat was a victim. She was raped by a man. She lost her life, but he stayed alive. Thus, the condition of Arab women needs to be reassessed. Arabs may need to find another thing to place their honor on. What does sex have to do with honor? It is a confused set of values in the Arab culture, or maybe misplaced value. For example, honor in the West is related to the ethical practices of an individual in their work in society, in the family, and among their fellow human beings.

Perhaps the Arab may need to come up with a different definition of the concept of honor. It can be the commitment of individuals to be good and helpful toward their fellow human beings. That can spare a lot of pain and agony.

We may also need a fundamental change in our attitudes and perceptions regarding the basic sexual need and respect it as a private matter. And if there is any violation, then the man needs to bear the consequences as well. The woman should not be blamed. She has endured much abuse throughout history and has been victimized for a long period of time as a result of our pathological attitudes towards her sexuality.

FAITHFULNESS

I visited Denmark in 1983. While I was in Copenhagen, I thought it would be a good idea to visit the tomb of Kierkegaard. He was a Danish philosopher and was considered one of the founders of the existential movement. While I was in graduate school in Colorado, I developed a keen interest in existential philosophy. Some of the sophisticated concepts of this philosophy are that there is no meaning to our existence and the accident of birth brought us to the world. We are born in a particular place, in a particular time, and under particular circumstances over which we have no choice. The ultimate absurdity is that we are born to die, we are condemned to be free, and we live an unauthentic life. Thus, we suffer from existential anxiety.

The philosophy thrived in the second half of the 20ᵗʰ Century, and I used the method in my psychological treatment of patients in my practice for many years. Jean-Paul Sartre and Albert Camus were also two of the originators of the philosophy along with Kierkegaard. However, Kierkegaard died at a young age of less than 40 years of age and did not see much in his life time. He did not even get married although he was in love with a woman who chose to marry a rich man, rather than a poor philosopher.

I took a taxi to the cemetery in the heart of Copenhagen so I could pay my tribute to that great man. While I was walking in the cemetery, I found an old man just sitting and I asked him, "Where is the tomb of Kierkegaard? He said, "Just go right, then take a left, and you will find it".

Out of my curiosity, I asked the man, "What are you doing here?" He told me was visiting the grave of his wife. When I asked him how long ago she had died, he replied, "Twenty years ago,"

I said, "So, you have not forgotten her."

He said, "No."

"How often do you visit her?" I asked.

He said, "Daily."

"You mean that you have been visiting her daily from 20 years ago until now?" He said, "Yes".

I asked, "Do you love her that much, or do you miss her?"

He said, "Both."

I said, "Please tell me your story," and he told me the following.

❖   ❖   ❖

I met my wife when I was around 26 years of age while I was working as a mailman in Copenhagen in 1926. Usually, I went to her house and delivered the mail, and she, not her mother or her father, used to come out to pick up the mail from me. I truly looked forward to delivering the mail to her house, and seeing her was the highlight of my day. It seemed that she developed an interest in me, and I developed an interest in her; her parents knew that. At that time, people used to be very conservative when it came to the relationship between a woman and a man.

One day I gathered my courage and asked her out. She said we could not do that unless I asked her parents. So, when I went to deliver the mail, I asked her mother. She said it would be fine, so I took her out to a local coffee house. At that time, Copenhagen was a very small town, and people knew each other. Mainly, everyone knew the mailman, Jack.

When I was with her, people always said "hello" to me. I noticed Silvia tended to get bothered by that, and she said to me, "I need your whole attention on me."

Our relationship became very close, and I felt I wanted to marry her, but at that point, I was not even able to kiss her because then people did not kiss, let alone have sex. Thus, I talked with my parents about her, and my parents supported that notion since I had a job and relied on myself. My father worked as a machinist in one of the small shops in Copenhagen, and my mother was a housewife, taking care of two bothers and two sisters.

My parents went with me, and we proposed to Silvia's parents. It was the happiest day in my life. Silvia and I went out daily to prepare for our wedding day, and our parents helped us.

The wedding day was set, and we got married. At that time, life was simple and not expensive. We were both having the time of our lives, a young couple that loved and respected each other. We lived an uncomplicated life, and there was satisfaction and contentment in our relationship. Our heads were empty of the rubbish of what we now call "civilization." Most of all, we had kindred spirits.

Silvia got pregnant, and we were so happy that we were going to have a family. Then, in her second trimester, she miscarried. We were both disappointed, but as Christians, we were thankful for what God gave us. Silvia did not work, but just took care of the house. She used to love to cook and invite our parents over. She was a great cook and truly put her soul into the food. She got pregnant again, and she miscarried again. We went to several doctors, but they did not know what happened. At that time, medicine was not as advanced as it is today. So, again, we felt very bad, but we left it up to God. Then she got pregnant a third time, and she miscarried, and the fourth time, as well.

I said, "My beloved Silvia, please do not try again. Let us be together without children." Our lives were so utterly good, and we enjoyed each other tremendously. We laughed a lot, and we played with each other like children. We also used to travel, but not a lot due to the nature of my job as a mailman. Silvia was a woman who liked to stay home and visit with her family and friends. My home was my kingdom, and Silvia made me feel I was the king in the home. That was the traditional value of that time, and it kept the family strong. She was a woman who always tried to bring out the best in me and never criticized me at all. We loved to be with each other all the time. The years passed, and we lived together a total of 20 years

Then one day, I came home and found Silvia lying down and not feeling well. At that time, Silvia had lost her parents, and she had just one sister left who was older than her. So, I called up her sister, and she came over. She brought some home remedy medicine and gave it to Silvia. However, her health did not improve, and we went to a doctor in Copenhagen. They did not know what was wrong with her. Silvia's illness lasted a few months, and it was hard on me to see her emaciated day after day.

One day she said, "Jack, do not go to your work today." I stayed with her, and she held my hand, and said, "Jack, life was so good with you, and I think I am leaving you today. I have a strong feeling that my journey on the earth and with you is coming to an end. But, please, do not leave me when I die."...

I asked, "What do you mean?" ...

She replied, "I want you to visit me often. I will be lonely in my grave and want your spirit to be around me even when I am dead." Then Silvia closed her eyes, held my hand, and died peacefully. It was the darkest day in my life, losing Silvia, so I buried her and I started to visit her almost daily for the next 20 years.

Normally, when I finished my work I would come here and talk to her about everything that had transpired during my day. She would often come to see me at night in my dreams and would tell me what to do. This has been going on for the last 20 years. I did not leave Silvia, and she did not leave me. In my dreams, her spirit is always with me, and I feel her wherever I go.

✤   ✤   ✤

Jack took a deep breath and said, "I wish I knew the day that I will die so I can tell Silvia goodbye.

I said, "You are not going to say goodbye because once you die, you will be united with her again. Jack, I have learned in the old books of religions that God normally brings to us in our next life to live with the person that we loved."

"Are you sure about what you just said?" he asked.

I said, "Yes. The spirit always goes in twins, and you will be with Silvia, and you will enjoy another chapter of your next life.

"Does our life have many chapters?" he asked.

I explained, "Yes, this is the first one that we live on the earth, and then we will go through many lives after this one."

He asked, "Are we going to be happy in our next life?"

I said, "It depends on what we do in this life. If you have set up from the start to be happy here, then you will carry that with you through the upcoming lives."

He said, "We are talking metaphysically here."

I said, "Yes, and I do not have scientific proof of what I am saying."

Then Jack said, "There is no need for scientific proof of human emotion and feelings. I can feel it, and I could sense it all those years with Silvia."

I said, "You are a very fortunate man to have a partner in spirit."

He said, "I thought most people did."

"No, most people do not," I said.

Then he turned his face to me and asked, "How about you? Do you have a partner in spirit?"

"So far, no."

He asked, "Then what does it take to have such partner?"

I said, "Jack, you and Silvia lived your lives through your heart, while I have no one because I am living my life through the gibberish in my head."

"Is there any difference?" he asked.

I said, "Of course. There is an ocean of difference between living your life through your heart and living your life through your thoughts and disturbance."

He said, "I enjoyed our conversation very much."

And, I said, "I will remember you Jack, always."

Then we exchanged phone numbers, and we hugged each other, and said goodbye. I called Jack from America once in a while and then started to feel Jack had developed Alzheimer's disease and had forgotten me. So, I stopped the calls.

⁙ ⁙ ⁙

The merit of this story is that there are some people in our world who are truly living life with immensity and simplicity. Perhaps, the basic ingredients for happiness in Jack's case were simplicity and being faithful to life in general. Jack lived a very faithful life to Silvia, and the rewards were so great that his life was a joyful journey, even though he was not aware of it. If he became aware of it then he would lose it. It is like walking in a garden and looking at flowers and beautiful trees and once you think how beautiful they are, you insert your thoughts, and that can take away the immediacy of the moment.

The sad fact of our existence nowadays is that we are not satisfied with what we have, but we are always looking for what we do not have. And that can make our life a miserable one. There is no contentment these days in our modern life. There is a strong urge to have more and more, and we do not cultivate a spiritual relationship with other human beings. As Kierkegaard said, "The age of anxiety does not allow you to derive a simple pleasure merely from daily existence."

EVERYTHING HAPPENS FOR A REASON

Since I left Detroit, Michigan, in 2002 to work in Abu Dhabi, I usually return in the summer season to spend time in my beloved hometown Detroit, with family and friends. Last summer, 2009, I went to Ohio to visit Anwar, who I call my cousin. He is an old man close to 90 years of age, and he is a friend of my father. My father has been deceased long ago, but he was so close to Anwar. He is a religious scholar, and he has many books in that respect. Once in awhile I will call him up from Abu Dhabi to check on his health. I really consider him like a father because he was very close to my farther. He even calls me Son Talib.

Normally, I visit him every year, but this year my visit was different than other years. I took him to a public park in Toledo, Ohio, and we had a heart-to-heart conversation. I asked him questions which were in my mind for many years, but did not dare to ask him even though I was so close to him. But, this time, I asked him, "Cousin Anwar, how did you lose your eyesight in your left eye?"

He said, "Son, that is a long story, and I will tell you all about it."

✣   ✣   ✣

I was born in the southern part of Iraq in late 1920 to a poor family. We were four brothers and two sisters, and I was the oldest one in the family. My father used to work as a fisherman in the marshes of Iraq, some of the most beautiful marshes in the world. At that time, life was very difficult for people to put bread on the table, and I had to work to help my father who had little money.

At age 13, my father asked me to help him out in the afternoons when I came from school. He asked a local barber in our village if I could work for him for a few hours a day. So, I started working with the barber, not cutting hair, just cleaning the place from the hair after each customer. And, sometimes, I would wash the hair of the customer. The barber liked me a lot, and I was doing an excellent job as well as getting some money to help the family.

At that time I was an extremely handsome boy, and I had big dark eyes. So, one day a customer came to get his hair cut. He took a deep look at me and said, "What beautiful eyes you have." He had just finished his sentence when I felt a sharp pain in my left eye. It was like a piercing needle in my eye. Within 10 minutes I was literally crying from the pain. The barber had to send for my father to come and get his son. (At that time there was no phone system in Iraq).

The barber looked at the man and said, "Why did you come today with your evil eye to my place and hurt the boy".

The man said, "I did not mean it.

By that time, my father came, and I was crying and telling my father I could not bear the pain, "Please take me to any doctor". Of course, there was no doctor at that time in the area, except for a local medicine man. So, my father immediately took me to him, and he looked at my eye and said there was nothing he could do for him. "He many lose his vision. Your son has been hit by an evil eye."

My father mentioned the name of the man who came to the barber ship, and the medicine man said that the man was very dangerous in our area. He had hurt many people by his powerful evil eye. Then the medicine man cited several stories about the man to my father and said, "Your son is not lucky to have met this man today."

The medicine man gave me some ointment just to sooth the excruciating pain. I was unable to sleep that night, and the next day I was unable to see with my left eye. I thought that maybe when the pain subsided that I would be able to see again. But, the next day, and the next 10 days, and the next month there was still no vision in my left eye. I had lost all of my vision in that eye and when I looked in the mirror, I saw my eye was just a white ball, with no dark part in it at all. I was scared and shook with a deep sense of loss for a part of my body.

My father and the rest of the village counsel got together and wanted to expel this man from our village because he had caused a lot of trouble for other people with his powerful eyes. They sent for him and said, "Please, you may need to leave our village." He accepted the decision and moved to another village. I heard later that he was kicked out of that village as well because of his evil eye.

I lost all of the eyesight in my left eye and now the right eye has started to get weaker. I finished high school, but with many struggles. People called me the blind boy, and I was degraded by the children often in the school because of my condition. In Iraq people often make fun of anyone who has some physical limitation and do not give any respect to people with such difficulties. Basically, it is a cruel society. However, that put down from others gave me some motivation to excel in my life.

Normally, in Iraq for a youth who reaches 18 years of age and finishes high school, there is mandatory army service. But, since I had a handicap condition there was a waiver from joining the army. So, I focused on my studies while my brothers, who had reached 18 years of age, had to join the army. Two of my brothers died in the war with the north. I was spared because of my physical limitation.

I became heavily involved in the study of religion and dedicated an inordinate amount of time towards that study. My star started to shine. Two of my brothers died in the war and a third one had just left the army and became a fisherman like my father. That was a very hard life to lead for him.

After the age of 27, I left my town and moved to the center of Iraq where the religious schools were located, and I enrolled there. I had gained notoriety by my knowledge and people came to study under my supervision. I published numerous books. At the age of 35 I moved to Egypt and got married, and had children. Finally I moved to our beloved land of America.

✦ ✦ ✦

So, Son Talib, if I had not lost my eyesight, I would have been in the army and I might have lost my life like my two brothers in one of the stupid wars that Iraq always wages. Or, I could even have done manual work in Iraq and never would have amounted to anything meaningful in my life. Son Talib, throughout these years I have cultivated myself intellectually, spiritually, and mentally, and worked to be a sensitive human being. Thus, I consider the loss of my eyesight a blessing for me. God took my vision, but gave me great health in this age and a highly developed mind. Son Talib, when you lose something in life, just be patient. Wait and see. There will be something good that comes out of it. One must know that nothing happens in the universe without a purpose or reason. The reason behind the loss of my vision was to accomplish scholarship and be an influential person who made a difference in the life of other people."

The merit of the story is that there is a hidden purpose behind everything that happens to us. The universe is purposeful, and nothing arbitrarily happens. The second observation is that there are no accidents at all. There is an invisible dynamic power that makes things happens. Moreover, our life is not ever complete because there is always something missing so that an individual is motivated to seek the completion of the missing part. And that is what makes our life challenging and meaningful.

Another observation about this case is that there are some people who are endowed with extraordinary psychic powers, and their vision can hurt as well as heal. The Russian people have done fabulous research in the field of parapsychology, while we in the West are still crawling when it comes to scientific explanations of such phenomena.

Our body and our psychic have incredible powers if we use them. The powers are beyond our five senses. The man in the village who hurt my cousin was a simple man who did not understand the inherent power that he had. If he was talking with people who knew about such powers, and if he had channeled his power, he would be able to heal people, rather then hurt them. Needless to say, we all have the power to heal ourselves and others if we know how to tap into such power.

The sad fact of the human condition all over the world is that the educational system and our parents are completely ignorant of our inner power. This is why our planet is so heavily populated with so many lousy, lazy and helpless people.

East is East . . . West is West,
The Twain Shall Never Meet

Oftentimes, there are strong arguments prevailing on many levels of society's thinking between the Middle Eastern and Western cultures. The core of the arguments is: *What is the difference between both cultures?* Arabs may think of themselves as backward people, or that they are behind the progress of the human community. Or, they may think of themselves as the descendents of the great civilization and have cavalier attitudes.

These arguments are much more pronounced among Arabs than the people of the West. I have lived in both cultures, but I hear it more often in the Arab culture. I would like to give my perspectives as a person who lives in both cultures and as a psychologist who specializes in the interpretation of human behaviors. However, I will try to shed some light on the nature of the differences of the two cultures. Even though the purpose of theses arguments is to develop some understanding and appreciation of both cultures, we are aware that there is a chasm between them.

The First Argument

Human beings are born with serious deficits whether in the East or in the West. For example, we are selfish, greedy, and aggressive by nature. God has sent many prophets to cultivate our nature. Some of us are cultivated beings and evolved spiritually, but the majority of us are still unable to transcend beyond our selfish mediocre nature.

In the West they have realized this fact about human nature, and they put in place a lot of laws to manage or control human greed; in the Middle East, however, we are left to our own desires or wishes or whims to be in control of ourselves. We see a lot of poverty in the Arab world even though we have a sufficient wealth. Perhaps, we do not have specific laws to regulate the human selfish tendency. For example, America has the highest number of legislators and institutions in the world to manage human behaviors. If we leave the human being to his own desire or wish, then he will eat alive the people around him, so to speak. It does not seem a romantic view of human nature, but that is the reality. People in the Arab world have an untamed ego; they like to have what their hands may hold. The Western society does not allow an individual person to wander around, letting his unbridled self take over the lot of his fellow human.

Our holy book, the Quran, spells out an insightful story about our human selfish nature. There were two brothers--one had ninety nine goats, and the other one had just one goat. The one with 99 wanted to have the one from his brother so he could have 100 goats, instead of 99. It is a clear indication of our innate human greed. The Western society trains people to follow the rules of law in order to control self-centered tendencies, while the Arab culture has not matured enough to go beyond oneself. Or perhaps, we do not have a specific mechanism to manage our greed. Thus, we are a massively self-absorbed people.

The Second Argument

The Arab culture is a fear-based culture. There are a lot of things that can initiate our fears. In the early years of our life, parents tend to insert tremendous fears of many things into us. For example, my mother used to put me to sleep and, if I did not want to go to sleep, she frightened me with the dark, with Jen, or even with fish; thus, I grew up afraid of the dark and of the fish. When a human being is raised up with such fears, do not expect him/her to be creative. Thus, we are behind the West in science and many fields of knowledge. Basically, we are fearful people. Our soul has been squashed by crippling fears, mostly the fears of others. Fears can also bring depression and make us unhappy and gloomy. If any individual operates out of fears, which can bring about all sorts of psychological problems. Perhaps they are not aware of the damage that they inflict upon their children when a family, a society, and a school all conspire to instill fears deep in our conscious or unconscious self.

However, Western society instills courage and hope in their children. The family or the educational system tries to produce a fearless person. Thus, Western individuals tend to experience a lot of adventures in their life. For example, they climb mountains and do all sorts of crazy things which make them very fascinating people. Consequently, the Western person can be creative and forward-thinking, while the Arab individual feels limited and confined by a lot of forces beyond his control. That is a marked difference between the two cultures.

As they say in the field of human motivation, a fearful person loses his role as an effective individual in life. If any individual feels he/she does not have control over his/her life, it can be very detrimental to his/her well-being. Arab people may also suffer from serious boredom, and sometime they may experience a meaningless existence. If you visit any Arab country and talk with the people, you will reach this sad conclusion.

The Third Argument

The Arab culture does not have an appreciation of the unique, special, or productive individual. It will try to assassinate him psychologically, or try to plot against him, or even to remove him from his place. A creative person might come up with new ideas, and that could be very threatening to the majority because it may show the inadequacy of the rest of us. Because such an individual may constitute a danger, and we have to get rid of him or her, a productive, creative, and sincere person may suffer in the Arab world. Thus, the majority of the scholars in the Arab world seek to live somewhere else and immigrate mainly to the West. They choose to live in the West because the West nurtures their creativity and uniqueness.

Moreover, in the Arab world a hard-working person with good intentions to make a difference may be humiliated and thrown out into the disposal. When you speak with people, you will hear a lot of stories supporting this argument. In other words, the Arab culture often *brings people down*. On the contrary, the Western culture *will often bring people up*. For many years I have worked in the West and have experienced this. If a person is unique and serious about making a difference, he will often be promoted and highly appreciated and rewarded for his dedication. Western society also will focus on productivity and enjoyment. They appreciate anyone who contributes to their development and good life. They use many ways to show you and acknowledge that you are a worthwhile being.

The Fourth Argument

The Arab society is a collectivist society, and the Western society is an individualistic society. What this means in a broad sense is that an individual in a collectivist society tends to drive his self-concept or self-esteem from his community, tribe, organization, and family at large. The individual cannot stand alone. His surroundings are more important then his personality. In other words, an individual in a collectivist society tends to build up the sense of self through the way he is seen in the community or through his place in society. However, in an individualistic society, of which most of the Western world is comprised, an individual tends to develop his sense of self through personal merit and achievement. In the end, regardless of the place of the family, an individual's self-concept is based upon his/her own hard work and accomplishments. Personal identity in the Arab world steams from many factors outside the individual self, while in the West, the identity is shaped by an individual's performance. This is a sharp difference between the two cultures.

We would all like to have a sense of belonging, but it is more pronounced in the Arab than in the Western culture. The individual in the Middle East society tries to work hard to please others so he/she can have society's approval. There are also established codes of conduct that individuals must never cross. At birth, the child finds the script already written that he/she must follow. Any violation of the codes can have serious consequences. But in the West, the individual is the one who designs his own code of conduct. This can be confusing at times, but it can also facilitate the creative part of the person. In the West an individual struggles to gain personal recognition, while in the Arab culture, he may inherit or merely be given recognition by his family.

The Fifth Argument

Perhaps related to the Fourth Argument (self-concept in an individualistic v. collectivist society) is that of individual appraisal. An individual in the Arab world tends to be appraised, or evaluated, or respected according to a set of unwritten roles. For example, having an influential family, wealth, and power, are factors that play a part in individual assessment. If a person has more wealth, or more power, or has an influential family, then he/she is respected accordingly. In the West, however, an individual's appraisal is based on personal accomplishment or on individual success.

Perhaps if we are critical in our view, we can see that there is a human element in the way the West looks at the individual because the assessment is based on who you are and what you have done as a human being. In the Arab culture, poor people with no strong family background and no power have limited opportunity. And, such an assessment can strip away an individual's humanity and dignity.

There is an ocean of difference between the two cultures. One culture promotes the skilled person and nurtures his creative self, while the other hinders an individual's spontaneity and stifles his soul.

The five arguments can characterize the prevailing aspects of the two cultures. However, I would like to make clear that no one culture is better than another. But, there are some features that differentiate one from the other. We just need to understand and be mindful of such differences. We must also try to identify the sets of limitations that arise with any culture's practices and see if such practices foster human creativity or deaden the soul. We must never make excuses for or apologize for certain cultural practices that might not facilitate human growth and dignity. We also have to acknowledge that the Arabs contributed greatly to the human community in many fields of science during the Islamic Renaissance. But since then, Arabs have lost the spirit of creativity and the art of giving. Perhaps, the only hope that we have lies in sincere self-reflection and reassessment to our strong hold on dogmatic beliefs about many things in our life. We also need to set our souls free.

THE CRUELTY OF FAMILY

I was attending The Arab Medical Conference in Dubai in 2006 when I turned to face a pharmacist who was in one of the conference promotion booths. I said, "Where are you from?"

She replied, "I am from Morocco."

At that time I was angry at Moroccan women because I was just divorced from my Moroccan wife. I said, "This is my number, and if you wish to call me, fine; and if you do not wish, just throw it in the trash can.

She said, "It seems that you are angry at something. Did I say something?"

I said, "Yes, I am angry at you Moroccan women."

She asked, "Why?"

I replied, "It is a long story, and I have to leave. Goodbye." I left her without even knowing her name or number, but she had my number.

That was in January, 2006. Then in March, I received a call from a woman. She said, "Talib, how are you?"

I asked, "Who is speaking with me?"

She said, "This is Zee."

"Who is Zee?"

She said, "I am the pharmacist from Dubai you met three months ago."

I said, "What has come to your mind to call me now?"

She said, "Your approach to me was different, and I am just carious to find out about your story with Moroccan women. And, I am coming to Abu Dhabi tomorrow. Can we meet?"

I said, "Sure, and welcome."

The next day Zee came by the bus, and I went to the bus station to pick her up. We went for dinner and then I said, "Can you stay with me tonight? And then you may go tomorrow." She said that it was a good idea. We went home, and I fixed up a drink for us. Then we started to talk and get to know each other. We indulged ourselves in lovemaking. She was a very hot woman.

The next day she had to leave, and I gave her a ride to the bus station. She called me the next day and said that she had enjoyed her visit with me and that she wished to see me the next week. I said, "Of course, welcome."

The following week came, and we started dating. Zee came every week. She would stay one night and then go back to her work in Dubai where she managed a pharmacy. She was a very proud woman and would never allow me to even pay her taxi fare. Our relationship was getting thicker, day to day. Either I called her, or she called me every day, and we really started to enjoy our conversations together. She was a very educated woman who spoke French, English, Arabic, and Russian languages.

Who was Zee? She was 33 years old, married once, and divorced. She grew up in Morocco and then got a scholarship to study pharmacy in Bulgaria. She lived for a few years in Paris with her sister who was married to a Frenchman. She opened a pharmacy in Rabat, the capital of Morocco. She was a very industrious woman, and she tended to rely upon herself for everything.

Our relationship was progressing, and we enjoyed our sexuality immensely. Zee was a woman with a strong appetite for sex, and once we got into it, we never finished. She wanted more and more. She had incredible skills in lovemaking, immersing her total self and giving and attending to the needs of her partner. I remember one night that Zee had 15 orgasms. The next day she was unable to even walk. She tended to like it a lot, although I thought Zee maybe was a nymphomaniac. She really wore me out. Sometime, I was unable to keep up with her tantalizing desire for sex.

She also liked to eat chocolate before lovemaking. She came home one night and lit candles, spread a white sheet on the floor, and said, "Tee (which she used to call me), this night is worth a million dollars. No one in this entire world is able to enjoy one another as much as we enjoy each other."

I said," Zee, you are one of a kind, and I really cherish you." God had given Zee a flawless body, and she was a dynamic woman.

We also used to spend time talking about different things in life, and Zee seemed upbeat. But, one day she broke into a crying spell, and I said, "Zee, please tell me." She said, "I do not want to upset you." And I replied, "I insist that you tell me about what is in your mind." She said, "Tee, just listen to me."

When I was 11 years old, I was playing on my bicycle on the streets of Rabat when a car came and hit me hard and smashed my face. As a result of the accident, there was some deformity on my face. But, my family did not treat me for it and kept me in the house with the deformity on my face. I always cried and asked my father to take me to a doctor to fix up my face. He refused, and he said that it cost money, even though he had money, and that he was from a middle class family. I stayed in the house, and they did not even send me to school. I started to beg him and my mother to let me go to school, so they sent me to school. Then I had to face the cruelty of the children who kept making fun of me and ridiculing me because of the deformity on my face. I became the center of jokes at the school, and I could not bear it. So my parents kept me home, but still they did not take me with them when they went out or traveled.

I stayed home by myself. I had four sisters and two brothers, and I was the middle one; all of them went out, except me. I cried, "Please take me," and they told me the ugly girl had to stay home. I was tormented inside hearing from my own family how what strangers would say.

There are two religious occasions that we as Muslims celebrate called Eid. My family tended to travel, but they kept me home. I cried my heart out and kissed their feet and hands, but no one in my family, not even my brother or sisters, had mercy in their hearts to listen to my pain of isolation. I lived with them, but they did not communicate with me at all. I stayed home from age 11 to age 17.

When a guest came to our home, they locked me up in a room, and they said they did not want the people to know that they had an ugly daughter like me. They were ashamed of me. I stayed in my room and cried and read books. When they slept at night, they woke me up, and I had to clean the house all night long so I would get tired and sleep during the day and they would not have to face me. Our house was a large one and cleaning up after eight people was not an easy task.

Needless to say, they did not allow me to go out of the house to meet any friends, so I did not have a friend. I started to develop severe depression and anxiety, and I did not even eat for days and days. No one in the family cared. My father even said, "Let her not eat so she can die, and we can get rid of her." When I heard my own father saying that, I felt worthless about myself. I really wished to die, but I knew I could not kill myself because I am Muslim, and Islam considers suicide a great sin.

None of our neighbors knew about me, and my relatives may have sometimes asked about me, but the family tended to avoid an answer and got upset if anyone mentioned my name. The torture, the pain, and the psychological abuses I endured from my own family were beyond human capability. I was imprisoned in my home. My solace was that God, one day, would free me, and I regained my hope in my life.

I stayed in this condition under constant torture by my family for six years. Then my older sister got married to a Frenchman, and one day he came to visit us. While my family was busy socializing, he accidentally stepped into my room. He found me and asked, "Who are you?"

I said, "I am your wife's sister."

He said, "I did not know that she had a sister. She never told me that you were her sister."

I said, "Yes. Look at my face and see that this is the reason they do not want to show me to the world."

He was furious, and outraged, and went to his wife and asked, "How in the world could you have a sister and not telling me, and we have been married for over six months! Are you ashamed of her?"

He went to my father and insulted him saying, "You have no ounce of humanity inside of your heart, and I want to divorce your daughter because I do not want to be related to such a cruel family."

I heard the conversation, of course, and at that minute my family wanted to literally wipe me off the face of the earth. So, I collected my courage, and stepped in, and in fluent French said, "Gentleman, my brother-in-law, I can see that you have compassion in your heart."

And, he said, "Of course. That is what I grew up with. We have to accept and love all people, no matter who they are, let alone a family member."

I continued, "Let me tell you that I have been in such a condition for six years. Please, I need your help right now. If you leave me with this cruel family, they will hurt me after you leave. I am living in a jungle, not with a family. So, please, be kind enough and take me with you to France and help me to have plastic surgery to restore the looks on my face."

He got my clothes out of the house immediately and took me to the hotel, and he stayed with me that night. The next morning, he arranged for my visa, and we took the first flight to Paris. He left my sister behind because he was upset and angry at the whole family. We went to his home in the suburbs of Paris.

He had a friend who was a plastic surgeon. He saw me and started to work on my face. The work lasted for a couple of months, and I went in on a weekly basis. There was a marked improvement in my face and looks.

My sister came, and we had a heart-to-heart talk, and I said, "Why did the family treat me like that? You would not even treat your enemy like that."

Naturally, she had no answer. I stayed in Paris for three years with my brother-in-law, and the relationship between me and my sister got better. I started to regain confidence in myself and finished high school in France. Then, I started to look for a job to help myself. I did not want to go back to my torturing place. I did not want to see my parents who had no compassion in their heart for their daughter. I found a job in a coffee house and started to support myself.

One day while I was working in the coffee house in Paris, I met a middle-aged Bulgarian man. He was a tourist, and we talked. I introduced myself to him, and he developed an interest in me. We went out together, and I became his tour guide. He asked, "Would you like to study in Bulgaria?"

And I said, "I would love it!"

"You have to learn the language."

"I will do anything."

He told me that he was the head of the pharmacy school at the University Sofia, Bulgaria. Then, he promised that he would send after me. After a few weeks, he sent me the papers for a scholarship to study pharmacy in Bulgaria. I left Paris. I was so happy that God had started to look after me and I could see the bright side of life after having lived with years of abuse from my own family. I stayed in Bulgaria for five years and got my doctorate in pharmacy, then went back to Morocco. I really did not want to live with my family, so I lived with a woman from Rabat who I met in Bulgaria while I was studying there.

Still, my heart was big enough, so I visited my family once in a while. I and the woman I was staying with decided to open a pharmacy in Rabat. She put up the capital, and I put up my degree, and we opened a pharmacy in a great location in Rabat. Now I had money, and my family started to come around. One of my relatives was a very poor man, and they wanted me to marry him so I could support him. I said, "No." But, I found the years were going by so fast, and I was a woman who loved sex very much. While I did not want to do it with anyone, I also wanted to have children, so I submitted to the pressure from the family and to my biological pressure and accepted the proposal of marriage.

I got married to him, and he found a job in Abu Dhabi. As a good wife, I had to go with my husband, leaving the pharmacy to be managed by my friend. We went to Abu Dhabi, and he found work with the police department, and I found work in a pharmacy. Then, my husband got into drinking every night, and he tended to be abusive if he drank too much. He started to beat me up, and even broke one of my fingers. I said, "This is the last thing that I need from marriage. I have been abused long enough," so I decided to divorce him. The divorce was final last month.

✢ ✢ ✢

"Now, as you can see, Tee, this is the painful story of my life. I am really thinking about getting married, and my hope is that you and I can have a family."

I said, "Zee, please understand that I just got out of a relationship and, psychologically, I have not healed yet. Thus, any marriage would be a rebound and, perhaps, would never last. Zee, you are a wonderful woman, but please just let us be friends."

She replied, "I must tell you, I need to have children, and the time is not serving me. My womb is crying for a baby."

Zee left me for a few weeks without any phone calls. I called her, but she did not answer. Then one day she called up and said, "Tee, can we meet for lunch?"

I said, "Of course, I'd be happy to see you."

We went to lunch, and then she showed me the papers of her marriage in the court to a man in Dubai, an engineer. I wished her the best of luck. I was very sad at losing her, and I have not seen her since that time. She also changed her phone number. I must say, the sexual compatibility between us was phenomenal and is greatly missed.

The merit of the story is that an Arab might sacrifice his or her own family member, or even themselves, for the sake of others--not for the goodness of others, but for social acceptance. They pay too much attention to what others may say about them, rather than how they feel. If a person focuses on pleasing others, then he/she loses the core of personality and becomes a puppet on the hand of others. Arab culture is a face-saving culture in which a person can do anything and go to any length just to be accepted by the community. Therefore, Arab individuals are in constant internal conflict, the conflict steaming between individual desires, wishes, needs, and societal approval and compliance. Normally, in such a climate, creativity is stifled.

That is why Zee's family acted in such a cruel inhumane way when hiding her so that the people or the neighbors did not say that they had a deformed daughter. Maintaining the façade is an embedded part of the Arab culture and that is why the culture is loaded with a lot of pathologies. The individual does not live in accordance with his/her personal nature; he has to take into account what others may say. The Arab culture needs serious development in their rational thinking to balance between individual needs and societal considerations. There is an old saying that an Arab individual lives a schizophrenic life. Such living makes the heart callous, and Zee's family is one example of such callousness, albeit, Zee's spirit has triumphed over all the odds.

Conversation with a Learned Man

I visited Cuba in 1999. Because, as we all know, American citizens are not allowed to visit the island country; I flew from Canada so Uncle Sam would not know about my trip. The island is one of the most gorgeous and happiest places on Earth. It has own charm, and there is a mystical quality about the island. That is why Cuba holds such a unique place among all the Caribbean Islands. The music and dance are woven into the fabric of the society. It is a place with such a positive energy that it makes you want to go back again and again. I was utterly in love with the island.

Normally, I take a walk every day just to explore a city and go to different parts of the town so I can see the authentic life of the people. I tend to engage in conversations with the people that I encounter on the roads.

One day I had lunch in one of the small restaurants, and after I finished eating, I felt a sharp pain in my stomach. I thought it might be a good idea to go to a hospital and find out why than to ignore it. Moreover, I learned that Cuba had the best system of medicine in the Caribbean hemisphere, so I went to the Havana Hospital located in the center of Havana. I entered the hospital and found a very attractive-looking female doctor there. I spoke to her, and she said she did not speak English, so she called on one of her follow doctors who did speak English. He came to me and spoke elegant English, besides Spanish. I explained my trouble to him, and he said, "Perhaps, there is some virus that you got from the food, but nothing is serious.

He was very curious to know about me and why I was visiting Cuba. "I am originally from the Middle East," I explained, "and for the last 30 years, I have adopted America as my home." Then I said, "Tell me about you."

He said, "As you can see, I am a general practitioner in this hospital, and I am in my mid-70s. I am retired, but I came here to handle certain cases, rather than staying at home and getting bored.

I said, "Since you are retired, are you done for the day?"

He said, "Yes."

I said, "How about I invite you to have coffee at the Hemingway Place?" Ernest Hemingway was an American writer who lived a large part of his life in Havana.

The doctor said, "Yes, let us take a walk to the place so we can have a Cuban coffee, which is considered the best coffee in the world." He explained that he had practiced medicine for over 45 years and enjoyed it very much, that he was a general practitioner, and he had seen thousands and thousands of people. He told me he loved every day of his work, and he had learned a lot from his patients--more than they learned from him.

He said he had kept a diary of the jest of the conversations that took place with his patients over all the years. I said, "Then you have a wealth of knowledge."

"Yes," he replied. "I owe a lot to them and am very thankful to my patients. They have even taught me how to live my life better and how to perceive things around me." He continued, "I normally give my patient enough time when they come to me, and I do not focus on the medications. I focus on their story and the totality of their being--mind, body, and spirit. My words are more important to them than my medicine. As Hippocrates, the father of western medicine, said, 'the word of the doctor has more cures than his medicines.'"

I said, "That fits me well because I am a psychologist who believes strongly in the power of words."

"Yes," he agreed, "words can heal you and words can make you ill."

I said. "Please, tell me the story of your life," and he did.

"I was married once, and my wife passed away after 35 years of being together. I have two sons who are adults and live by themselves. I went to the Havana Medical School, and I have been practicing since then."

I asked, "Do you live by yourself?"

He replied, "Yes, and I enjoy it."

I asked, "Do you feel lonely at times?"

He replied, "Of course. This is the age of loneliness."

"Are you happy?" I asked....

He replied, "Very much."

"What is making you happy?"

He replied, "Helping my patients and making them feel well, doing good for the universe, but most of all, I do not dance around myself. I am not centered on my Ego."

I said, "It seems that you have wisdom in your life and that you are a wise man."

"You might say that," he replied. He was sipping his coffee, and I could sense that his eyes were open to the enjoyable conversation. He continued, "I like to challenge my mind always so that my mind stays active and sharp. Otherwise it would become dull. If you do not use it, you will lose it; it is like any organ in our body."

"What is the most important thing that you have learned from your patients?"

He said, "That everything will come to pass. Do not worry because tomorrow there will be sunshine and because 90% of our worries never happen."

I asked, "Do you have judgment or conclusions about certain things in life?"

"Life is as it is, whether you like it or not. Just live it fully. And, do not live it from your mind, live it through your heart, and you will be happy."

"Do you see the beauty in the world?" I asked.

He replied, "I do, but the majority of us do not because our minds have been cluttered with worry and fears."

I asked, "What are the most common fears you have noticed in your patients?"

He said, "The fear of others and the fear of the unknown. And," he said, "As you know, Talib, most of the fears are imagined ones, not real ones."

I asked, "What do you like to do most?"

He replied, "Just take a walk and look around the town of Havana, or look to the endless sea around us. And, reading can be very fulfilling for me, and the interaction with positive friends can be very soothing to me."

"Do you enjoy food?"

He said, "Yes, the healthy kind; however, some of my patients are suffering from serious obesity, and this is why we have seen a sharp increase in the cases of diabetes. Food became a source of comfort for them, rather than a source of nourishment. Moreover, there is an abundance of food in the world, and some of us have more than what we need, while the rest of our follow humans are starving."

I questioned him, "Based on your contacts throughout the years of your practice, what do you think of people in general?"

He replied, "Every single individual on the face of the earth is greedy, selfish, aggressive, lazy, and mediocre by nature, unless they cultivate their nature." And then he exclaimed, "Talib, how many people have you met in your life who are cultivated human beings?" ....

I said, "Just a few." Then I asked, "How can we cultivate our nature and transcend above what you have just described?"

He replied, "Just have an inner understanding of what is inside of you and of what your ulterior motive is in your own actions or thoughts."

I said, "It seems that you are drawing a gloomy picture about human nature."

He replied, "I did not draw it; it has been drawn by the Almighty God since the creation of mankind when Adam committed the grave mistake, and that was a great disappointment to God."

I said. "It seems that you are angry."

He said, "Even God got angry and flooded the whole earth and drowned the human race. Talib, anger is a part of our human nature, but it can also be cultivated and channeled to become a positive force for change."

I asked, "What is peace?"

He replied, "The most important part is inner peace."

"How can you achieve it?

He replied, "By understanding the complexity of an emotion and trying to direct it by proper perspective, rather than projecting it onto others, as well as recognizing and accepting the two parts of the self; the demonic part and the compassionate part."

Then I asked, "Has it ever happened that you disrespected yourself on an occasion?"

He said, "Many times. When I say something that I do not believe, or just say it to please others, or do something out of fear, those are the times when I really disrespect myself."

I asked, "What do you think of money?"

He said, "It can be the seed of evil, and it can be the source of good deeds. It depends on the individual. One can either treat it as a master, and then it will take all the happiness from you; or one can treat it as a means, and then you can manage living expenses. Money may bring happiness, and it can be the source of misery.

"This statement is very true," I said. "Money can tap into the corner of our human greed; consequently, that can devour the joy out of our life."

"What is the best capital that you have?"

He responded, "It is the wisdom of learning from my own experiences and the experiences of others, but we never do. We are just like an addict who does not learn from others' or from his own mistakes."

I asked, "Why do we like to go into the past?"

"It is human nature that we have nostalgic tendencies. It can be meaningless.

I said, "Now, what do you think of sex?"

He said, "It is the greatest pleasure that God endowed us with."

"Do you do it with anyone?"

He said, "You may have it with people who you love, or you may have it with a total stranger. It is like a home-cooked meal or a fast-food meal. You need them both at times. But," he continued, "do not put too many thoughts into sex. It is a pleasure. Just flow with it, and enjoy it."

I asked, "Why did God create us?"

He said, "It is a preparation for our eternal life." He continued, "There will be many lives after this one. This is not the only one."

I asked, "What does generosity mean to you?"

He responded, "It is the generosity of the heart--when you give from your total being, when you are compassionate towards others, when you are kind enough to do things without expecting in return."

I asked, "Are you a negative person or a positive person?"

He said, "Overall, I am positive because being negative can drain your energy and leave you an empty dry person."

I asked, "Are you critical of others?"

He said, "Yes, when it comes to injustice and unfairness."

"Why do we have so much war and killing in the world?" I asked.

He said, "Remember this is human nature. Our father, Cain, killed his brother, Abel."

I asked, "What is the most difficult task any human can face?"

He replied, "Raising up children, and the majority of us are fabulously ignorant about it."

I asked, "Do you control yourself all the time?"

He said, "I do most of the time, but when it comes to a beautiful woman, I tend to lose it."

"Why?"

"I am a very visual man, and I appreciate the beauty a lot." He looked at me and said, "I am savoring every minute of our conversation; it's very appealing to me."

I asked, "What do you think of death?"

He replied, "There is no death, from either scientific or religious perspectives. There is a transformation from one form to another."

I said, "Do you sleep well?

He said, "Most of the time, and I enjoy it a lot."

I asked, "Have you ever cried?"

"Yes, when I lost my wife," he replied. "She was my true partner and supporter."

I asked, "What do you think of freedom?"

He responded, "People do not want to be free. They like to be in bondage and they give lip service to it. Freedom means responsibility."

"What do you think of love?" I asked.

He said, "We cannot live without love. It is the ultimate force that keeps this world running."

"Have you been in love?"

"Yes, many times, and it is the best feeling anyone can have."

"Do you listen well to your patients?"

He said, "It is the best gift that one can give anyone--when you stop your mental dialogue and attend totally to them."

I asked, "What do you think of women?"

He responded, "The soul is neither male nor female, and our body does not define us. We all are creatures of a loving God. However, women are not emotional beings as the common belief professes. They are very pragmatic and realistic creatures. They are the breath of life."

I asked, "What does patience mean to you?"

He replied, "It is a great virtue that we must have."

Then I asked, "What is the human dilemma in our present time?"

He replied, "Humans are missing the target or the purpose of being on earth [which is to be happy& healthy], and they are driven by irrational forces in their lives."

"What is life in general?"

He said, "It can be a fruitful journey, or it can be a meaningless one, it depends on what we put into it. Life is like a juicer. If you put in an apple, then you get apple juice; if you put in carrots, then you get carrot juice. If you put in good, you get the good." In other word you get what you put in.

And, he continued, "Please, be mindful of this fact." He said," We have to share what we have in our reservoir. Thoughts can be contagious; thus, we have to watch what we say and do. It can affect everyone around us."

"How about injustice?"

He said, "Man has committed a lot of injustices against himself as well as against others. It started when our father committed the grave mistake of disobeying God."

I asked, "What do you mean?"

He explained, "God is the omnipresent and the manifestation of all the good in the world, but we tend to disregard all of those manifestations. Our nature is a defiant one. Oftentimes, we work against ourselves."

"Why is that? I asked.

He responded, "Through my practices I have found that people do not follow the basic rules of good health, even if they know they are very beneficial for them."

I asked, "How about music?"

He replied, "The food of the soul and humanity is progressed through music and art, not through technology."

"Do you have computer?"

"I do not need another gadget that controls me. " I try to live my life with simplicity and contentment."

"Speaking of medicine," I said, "since you have been a doctor for such a long time, do you think we are overdoing it?"

He replied, "Yes. I tend to tell people when they come to me, please let your body heal itself. It has the potential to heal by itself, but we tend to disable our immune system by pouring into our body all these medications. For example, antibiotics can be a great medicine, but we are overdoing it." He continued by saying, "Health is a full-time job, and most of us say, 'I do not have time to exercise or select the proper food.' I believe strongly as Hippocratic said, 'Let your food be your medicine.' Then I tell my patients, 'If you do not have time for health, then you will have time for illnesses, you will miss a lot of days by being sick.'"

I said, "Doctor, I am very perplexed by human nature is that people oftentimes know the right way, but they do the opposite anyway."

He said, "Talib, people in general are fabulous idiots, and they do not know the art of living." He continued, "Living is an art and requires a lot of skills to be mastered although the painful fact is that the majority of us do not have a clue about the art of living. Or even if we know, normally, we do not follow."

Then I said, "Doctor, perhaps as the sage man, Sigmund Freud, wrote, our death instinct is stronger than our survival instinct."

Finally, I said, "It seems that you are a man with great intelligence and a wealth of knowledge."

He said, "Please Talib, intelligence means the ability to live life joyfully. Otherwise you are an absolutely stupid person. As far as knowledge, it means that you have the ability to know how to solve problems at all levels."

I said, "People these days are depressed, and perhaps depression has become the number one illness in the world."

He responded, "Our life is going too fast. Mankind is not able to cope with so much advancement in such a short time. Our nervous system is not designed to take in all the stimuli that we are bombarded with daily. We are still designed for the hunting and gathering era of our time. And, most of all, we are not living in accordance with our nature as Erich Fromm indicated in his book, *To Have or to Be*.

"So, then what is the answer?"

He said again, "We have to stop greed. 'It is a new form of insanity that is controlling us,' as Spinoza said. And, be satisfied with a little. Look at us in Cuba. We have little, but we are, overall, a happy people.

Then I looked at him and said, "Give me a word of wisdom which you have learned from your practice or from your life that can guide me."

He replied, "Have balance in your life between your physical needs, spiritual needs, psychological needs, and mental needs. Also, be forgiving of yourself and of others. And, most of all, try to live your day as if it was the last day for you on the earth through the nourishment of being giving, and receiving."

PSYCHOLOGICAL POLLUTION

We are all hurt by environmental pollution, but have we thought about psychological pollution? First of all, we may need to define pollution. Webster's Dictionary defines pollution as: impure, dirty, making things unclean, corrupt, contaminate, filthy, and desecrate. Needless to say, we are living in a polluted world because we are greedy and want to get everything fast and easy without an ounce of care about our earth. We dumped everything into our rivers, lakes, and sea and onto our land. We built up factories all over the world, but we did not look at ways we could protect our environment. However, we are becoming aware of the damage that we caused to our environment, and there are some movements nowadays to pay more attention to our environment because we are getting sick a lot.

However, psychological pollution can be more dangerous than environmental pollution. The primary contributor to psychological pollution is war and the killing of people. When there are killings in a certain place, the place becomes polluted, and the dark energy tends to cover up the place. Consequently, the living conditions of people become difficult and can be nerve-racking. When a person is killed, the energy of the body and the spirit may stay attached to the place. Thus, the collection of many killings in one place can attract another killing, polluting the whole place. As they say, killing attracts killing. That is what happened in Philistine, Afghanistan, Iraq, and parts of Africa. Those places are infested with blood, and that can be a magnet for more killing. As a result, the evil forces may take over. Since energy cannot be killed, only the physical part of the body, the energy does not leave the place. So, killing human beings can have the utmost detrimental effect upon the psychological climate of the place, and it may last for several years.

Hence, we may need to clean these places of psychological pollution through establishing a civil society based on respect for the sanctity of life. For example, European countries have been in horrible wars, but now have stopped the killing and are building a society based on acceptance of others' differences. What is needed in Afghanistan, Iraq, and Philistine is to stop the killing and begin a major cleaning of their souls by accommodating the different views among themselves.

Another part of psychological pollution is the negative energy that people may carry. For example, if a person is depressed, the molecule of his breath is in the air, and everyone can breathe it in and get infected like the transmission of other infections. Soon, we could all suffer from a blue mood, depression, anxiety, phobia, aggression, or envy and engage in negative talk about others.

All these are contributors to the production of psychological pollution, and it can affect any person without ever being aware of it. For example, have you been in a place and felt nervous and wanted to leave right away? I am sure you have. Perhaps that place had an accumulation of negative energy because thoughts, words, and actions have energy that can stay in a place; then, you feel it. That is why one needs to be very careful about the process of one's thinking and one's actions and behavior because they can have a profound impact on others as well as on the individual him/herself.

Psychological pollution can also be the result of interactions between an individual's surroundings and the individual. For example, if we live in a crowded area, the chance of having trouble is greater than if we live in an open space. Cement buildings are very unhealthy for us, and perhaps wood is better because wood is closer to nature. It is not synthetic, and synthetic things can have negative interactions with us. For example, modern cities across the world are not healthy places to live because developers poured a lot of cement with little attention to planting trees. That is why crime can flourish in a big, crowded city, while living in the countryside can be a more relaxing place.

Psychological pollution is contagious. We are all one human community, whether we live in Brazil or in India, so if something happens to a person in Brazil, there is no doubt that a person in India can be affected. For example, if a person is suffering from flu, the air can transfer the illness to other parts of the world. Thus, the physical health of people around the world is a matter that concerns all of us because we all share this small planet Earth, and if someone has something harmful, it can transfer to another person in a different part of the world. There is no one immune from such interaction. We do not live in isolation. Even the person who lives in a remote village in Egypt can be hurt by the depression of one person in Oman.

Psychological pollution is difficult to clean up because it requires many generations of people to follow the path of peace and positive energy. While we can use modern technology to clean up environmental pollution, how do we clean up psychological pollution? For example Afghanistan, is a place with no natural resources. It is a barren land of mountains and a lot of rocks, and the place has been infested with psychological pollution as a result of the loss of many lives. And, that attracts more and more killing. How do we clean it up? The first step that people must take upon themselves is to stop hurting each other, and that may require a different level of awareness than what they have. As Albert Einstein said, "Problems cannot be solved at the same level of awareness that created them." We may need a different level of awareness and understanding--the awareness that human life is worthwhile. If a person carries a different opinion than mine, it does not mean that I have to eliminate him or her. But, this is exactly what is happening in Afghanistan, Iraq, and Philistine. People do not tolerate differences.

What might be the solution? The educational system might play a crucial role in educating people that differences can be very healthy for human growth, rather than a reason to end the life of others. The key to cleaning up the psychological pollution is education, but what kind of education? Perhaps it is the kind of education and awareness that makes people transcends the dark side of their self and accepts others as partners with whom to share the earth.

Conclusion

Psychological pollution can be a breeding ground for evil forces to prevail. Psychological pollution hurts all of us, not just those in the place where it grows. This is why it is imperative that all of us get involved and correct the trend of violence that we observe in places around us. We also need to instill a sense of compassion in our children so that when they grow up, they do not participate in psychological pollution.

Moreover, our journey is limited to a number of years on the planet Earth. Thus, our responsibility is to live in peace within ourselves as well as with others. Of course, that is easier said than done. So, what do we do? As Albert Einstein indicated, we need to create and foster a high level of awareness among people, in general, to appreciate each other and weed out the ugly face of humanity.

THE WOMAN FROM BRAZIL

Sam, a middle-Eastern man, immigrated to America from Iraq in 1977. He worked very hard to be something in the "land of opportunity." He finished his higher education and became a highly professional and very educated man. He excelled and accomplished in his field, and he became an outstanding member of the professional community. Still, he felt empty inside and struggled to find the meaning in his life. He tended to ask the questions: Why are we here in this world? Why did God create us? Does God really need us to worship him? Why are children dying of starvation? Why are people cruel towards each other? How can a human being lose his humanity and hurt others intentionally? Why is there so much greed and pure selfishness in the world? Is the nature of the human being good or bad? All of these philosophical questions roamed through Sam's mind. And, once in awhile, he suffered from bouts of depression as a result of his struggle to find the meaning in his life.

He started to travel and wander around the world. In his travels, he often would indulge himself with the thrill of having sex with different women. He felt happy and considered these as peak experiences in his life. Perhaps, our beloved father, Freud, would analyze this as Sam searching for the missing love of his mother who had divorced his father when he was five years old and married another man. Sam grows up a lonely child in the house of his father who remarried, as well; and the step-mother was very inconsiderate of Sam. He lived a life with neither support, nor care, nor attention from his father or the rest of his family. Sam carried that and buried it in his unconscious mind.

The travel and sex became a tranquilizer for him. He felt very elated when he had sex with a strange woman. Sam tried to meet the thinkers and the scholars of each country he visited and learn from them the meaning of life. But, of course, each of us tends to define that meaning from our own perspective.

Sam visited over 100 countries around the world. In 1982, on one of his trips he took an airplane from Buenos Aires, Argentina, to Recife in the northern part of Brazil. The gentleman who was seated next to him on the airplane was a Brazilian man with a very distinguish personality. During the conversation that took place between them, the Brazilian man asked Sam, "What do you like to do in your visit to Recife?"

Without any hesitation, Sam responded, "I would like to see the city and have sex with different women."

The Brazilian man laughed a lot and said, "I can help you in that, and I will show you the time of your life. I will take you to a special, wonderful place to enjoy sex with different women." Sam was delighted and very happy that this man would take him to such a place.

The airplane landed in Recife. The Brazilian man took a special interest in Sam and found him to be a very fascinating man. He took Sam to his home for lunch and introduced Sam to his wonderful family. Then, after lunch, the Brazilian man drove Sam outside of the city, and they reached a huge, gated villa surrounded by thick trees. It seemed they knew him well at the gate and respected this man. They opened the door for him and greeted him with much reverence.

The Brazilian man talked to them in Portuguese and asked them to take good care of Sam and told them he would come back after five days to pick him up. The people in the villa paid special attention to Sam and took him around to show him the facility. But most importantly, they showed him seven of the most beautiful women any human could ever see in a lifetime. It seemed the villa was a high caliber brothel. They informed Sam that he was a guest there, and that he could drink, eat, and have sex with any of the women. Sam was in seventh Heaven, like a child in a candy store. The place had a movie theater, a swimming pool, a restaurant, and everything that one might imagine—as well as the seven most gorgeous women in Brazil.

Sam enjoyed his time and had unlimited sex with all the women during the five days. But, he felt his heart began to grow towards one of them in particular, and her name was Christina. She was gorgeous and tall and she could take your breath away and never give it back. And she had an incredible spirit that attracted the goodness in everyone. She had an impeccable body with bronze skin. Sam and Christina started to spend a lot of time together and talked about the meaning of life. It seemed that Christina was struggling with the same thoughts as Sam: "Why are we here on the earth?"

Moreover, Christina talked with Sam about her dreams in which she had always wanted to do something meaningful in her life to help others or her family, but she had no education or money. She had a great spirit and a heart of gold. She just wished the good for everyone in her life. She had the heart of a child who doesn't know how to lie or say bad things about anyone. Sam used to call her Angel--but in the body of a tiger when it came to sex. She invested her total self in the act of sex, and she gave the whole of her being when she made love to Sam. Sex between them became more than physical satisfaction, it was like a spiritual journey that both of them took to reach the stage of Nirvana in the Hindu religion. Christina and Sam had strong sexual appetites. There was a strong mutual attraction between them, and they spent the five nights together, talking about many things in their lives. Their thoughts were very similar to each other, and both of them were searchers, wanting to do good for others.

The time came for Sam's friend to pick him up and return to Recife. But, by then, the bond and the love between them had grown so strong that Sam and Christina had agreed to get married. Sam had always wished to marry a prostitute, and now he had found Christina who met these criteria. She was working in a brothel and was a wonderful human being.

The love between Sam and Christina was very strong, and Sam left the villa with the promise that the two of them would get married. After he sorted out a few things in his life, he would bring Christina to America. Sam told the whole story to his Brazilian friend, and the old man blessed the union. He said, "Listen, Sam. This can be a marriage made in Heaven." And, Sam flew back to America, his heart growing ever fonder of Christina.

Sam talked to Christina daily on the phone. He made all the arrangements very quickly and brought Christina to America. He introduced her to his family. And, although the family was very disappointed because his older sister wanted him to marry a Middle Eastern woman, but they gradually began to accept her.

Christina had a major goal for their marriage. She wanted to study and get an education so that she could help her family and the women with whom she had lived with in the brothel. She was a woman with a mission— she wanted to get a degree and make some money so that she could free the rest of the women from the brothel lifestyle. Sam was supportive of her goal, and he got her into a college to get a degree in finance. Christina attended Wayne State University in Detroit, Michigan. There, she excelled in her studies and became an honor student and scholarship recipient. She graduated with a degree in finance and a 4.00 GPA.

Needless to say, the love between Sam and Christina grew very deep. Christina got pregnant twice, but, sadly, miscarried each time. They both wished to have a child to share, but it seemed that God had another plan. Christina got a job in a big finance firm in Troy, Michigan, and she started to make very good money. She saved her money to complete her mission, to help her family and the girls in the brothel in Brazil.

For family, Christina had only her loving mother who lived in Recife. Sadly, she received the news that her mother had become paralyzed and had no one to take care of her. Christina had a very strong bond with her mother, and she wanted to spend time caring for her. Christina and Sam were then faced with making new arrangements for Christina to go to Brazil and find a job in Recife in order to be close to her mother. Of course, this was very difficult for Sam, but he had to look at the situation from the humanitarian side. Christina's mother was dying and had no one to care for her, and Christina would feel guilty if she was not near her mother.

So, Christina and Sam flew to Brazil. Sam spent some time with Christina's mother, who was a very spiritual woman, before returning to America.

Christina was a very bright woman and wanted to help her friends in the brothel. She opened a printing company and brought all the girls from the brothel to work for her there. Because Christina believed strongly that education was her salvation, she stipulated that part of their salary must go toward taking different educational courses at the local university in Recife. Her printing company became big and generated a lot of profit.

During this time, Christina lost her mother, which was very painful for her. Sam normally went to Brazil every three or four months to spend time with his beloved wife, but began to sense that a change was taking place inside Christina's heart. He asked her, "What is happening?"

She did not know what to say. To her, it seemed that the distance had done terrible things to the relationship, and she grew distant from him. Once again, Sam was very emotional and could not accept that his beloved wife, his soul mate, and his companion had drifted apart from him.

Sam returned to America, wearing his heart on his sleeve. His whole family said, "We told you so." The phone contact between Sam and Christina became minimal, and Sam was unable to find out what had happened to their relationship. Christina was very depressed, and she was unable to tell him that she had lost her love for him, that the death of her mother made her very depressed, and that she had even lost her desire for any sex.

Christina asked for a divorce, and Sam thought, perhaps, there was another man in her life. But, the women who worked for her respected Sam a lot and reported that there was no one in her life at all. Out of respect for Christina, Sam granted her the divorce through the Brazilian court. It was the darkest day of his life. All the women who worked with Christina were deeply saddened because they truly loved both Christina and Sam.

So, Sam flew back to America. There, he went for serious psychotherapy and started to take the medication Xanx to sleep. He was severely depressed and had no answer to what had happened to his relationship. He talked to Christina once in awhile, and sometimes he talked to her staff. The staff reported that Christina was growing isolated and did not like to take care of herself and she was not even bathing. Christina, the clean, elegant, beautiful creature, was losing the meaning in her life. Sam insisted that the woman who worked with her take her for some treatment, but Christina refused. Gradually, Christina did not leave her home and neither was she eating or sleeping.

One day Sam received a phone call from her staff saying that Christina had committed suicide. She had not come into work for two days, and the women went to her home and found her dead. Sam was shocked and despondent. He flew to Brazil, and the autopsy there indicated that Christina had taken an overdose of a tranquilizer. Her heart had stopped.

Her death remains a mystery to everyone who knew her. Sam and the women buried her. The printing company was taken over by her friends, the women who had worked with her in the brothel. They established a foundation in her name allocated part of the profits of the company to scholarships for any prostitute who wanted to get out of that business.

This was a real story. The events took place from 1982 to 1992.

PSYCHOLOGICAL INCEST

It was October, 1999. I was the keynote speaker at an international conference in Ann Arbor, Michigan. After my speech two women came towards the podium and told me they enjoyed the speech. One of them was Wafa, the wife of my friend and an immigrant from Iraq. Then, I asked Wafa, "Who is this gorgeous woman with you?"

She replied, "This is Sana, my niece, who just came from Syria. She left Iraq because of the political situation. She lived in Syria for awhile, and now she came to America.

I said to Sana, "Welcome to America," and she smiled in return. Then we engaged in small talk, and I said, "How about we all go to lunch next week?"

Wafa responded, "That is a great idea. Just call us."

There was a special aura about Sana, and after a few days, I called up Wafa and we all went to lunch. Wafa suggested that since I was divorced and Sana was divorced and without children that the two of us get together, just to get to know each other, leaving the rest to God. Actually, I was hoping for that. So, we exchanged numbers, and I called up Sana after three days.

We had a very good conversation and dinner, and we agreed that we would try to see each other. I started seeing her almost daily and we spent time talking about different things in our lives. She had an opinion about everything in life, and she could manage a great conversation.

Who was Sana? She was over 30 years of age, and had finished her

Liberal Art's degree from Baghdad. She got married to a school teacher who lived in Tunisia and lived with him one year, then asked for a divorce. She did not tell me the reason. She was a strikingly beautiful woman and went back to stay with her family in Baghdad. She was the oldest in the family. Her father had died three years before from bone cancer. It seemed she was very close to her father. He was a very prominent man in the Iraqi government, and was in a very close circle to the rulers. After his death, the family had to leave Iraq, and they were scattered around the world.

She also informed me that she was engaged to an Iraqi man in Syria, but the man suddenly died. According to Sana, he died of a heart attack. She was disappointed by her fiancé's death.

We started dating each other and spending time together. Then Sana asked to move in to live with me. Of course, I was very delighted to have her beside me every night. However, Sana seemed depressed, and her mood could change drastically without any obvious reason. I figured out that she was not a happy woman. I thought that it was because she had just come to this country and an immigrant is normally depressed during their first year. Or, perhaps it was because she had just lost her fiancé' in Syria, or she remembered her father.

Then, Wafa, her aunt, reminded me, "Talib, you have been going together for two months, and you may need to make an official engagement because the people in the community may start to talk about both of you. And, we all know that Middle Eastern people are strict when it comes to dating and a woman's honor."

Wafa took it upon herself to make the engagement official and invited some of our friends over for a little engagement party for us at her house. I took flowers for everyone who attended the party, and we all read some verses from our holy book, the Quran. Then, we were officially engaged. We started to feel close to each other, and we even engaged in sex. Sana liked sex a lot, and we used to spend the whole weekend just playing with each other.

One day as I was looking for my car keys, I asked, "Sana, where are the keys?" and she answered with such big laughter that she had thrown the keys in the sewage system. I asked, "Why did you do that?"

She said, "Just to see your reaction. If you got upset, then you do not love me, but if you did not get upset, then you love me."

When I asked if that was her test of love, she said, "Yes," so, I did not make anything out of it and thought that, perhaps, she had seen it on one of those stupid dating game programs on TV.

One day I took Sana to a revolving restaurant in Detroit in the GM Building downtown. We had dinner, and she was upset with me. When I asked her what the problem was, she said, "I feel like I want to throw myself from this building and end my life."

I said, "Are you joking?"

She said, "I mean it."

"Why?"

She replied, "I just do not like my life without my father."

I said, "You told me your father died three years ago."

She responded, "I still remember him, and he was everything in my life."

I said, "That is wonderful, but it seems that you have not overcome your grieving over the death of your father." And then I asked, "Beloved Sana, can you please tell me the whole story of your relationship with your father?"

She explained.

"I was the first girl to him, and I am prettier than my mother, so when I became a young girl at age 12 years, he started to take me out alone without my mother. We would go to restaurants and other places, and we really enjoyed each other very much. When he used to come from work, he would come to my room. And, I would bring him his lunch and he would eat with me. We kept my mother away in the other room. My relationship was very close with him. Even when he dressed up in the morning to go to work, I had to choose his clothes for him, and then he would kiss me goodbye. He did not do that to my mother. Then, my mother started to feel jealous of our relationship, and she started to hate me and fight with me all the time. When he used to travel, I could not go to sleep unless I brought his clothes to me so that I could smell them. Only then could I go to sleep."

"We used to get invited to different places because he was high up in the government ranks, and he would often take me along and did not take my mother. I was supposed to study in the city of Basra in the southern part of Iraq after I finished my high school, but I was unable to separate from my father. However, I did finish at my Liberal Art's school."

"He also used to take me out to buy clothes, and he tried them on me, and I used to wear what he liked me to wear. I normally would choose his clothes as well. Our relationship was inseparable."

"However, the tense relationship between me and my mother lead to an attack on me with a sharp object by my mother. My father was not in the home, so when he came home, he sent my mother to her family, and she stayed with her family over eight months. That was the best time of my life with my father."

I kept listening to her story without judgment or interruption to see how far that man had gone with his daughter. And she continued.

"All the girls in school envied me about my close relationship with my father. I really miss him a lot, and I do not know how to live without him."

I said; "Sana, we are engaged, and I am going to be your man."

She said, "You cannot take the place of my father. He was a very exceptional man."

I asked her to describe him to me. She said, "He was a very kind and considerate man. He used to give me everything I wanted and never said 'no' to me. He used to write poetry about my body and about how beautiful I was. If my mother or any members of my family wanted anything from him, they had to go through me. He would not give them anything unless I said so. In reality, I was running the house and I even had power over him. He would not do anything unless he consulted with me and got my approval."

"Sometimes there were very sensitive matters related to his work, and he would often ask for my opinion. And, normally, my opinion was the best."

"Then he got really sick and was hospitalized in Baghdad for bone cancer, and I stayed with him for over four months. He died at the age of 49. He was a very young man and since his death until now, my life has been shattered. After his death, I was hospitalized for a month or so. He was an ideal man. He used to adore me and he worshipped the ground that I walked on. It is impossible to forget him. May he rest in peace?

"After his death my relationship with my mother got better, but my siblings do not like me. And, I do not like myself after the death of my father."

Then she looked at me and said, "I want you to play the role of my father."

"What am I supposed to do," I asked.

She said, "You need to give me anything that I ask for, and you also need to involve me in every detail of your life."

I said. "Tell me more about your life."

She continued, "Normally I do not stay with a man if he does not act like my father."

I asked her how many men she had been with, and she said, "I was engaged 15 times. Once I go out with a man and he says that he will not act like my father, I have to leave him."

After I heard the story of Sana, I said to myself, "What a mess I have put myself in." But I had grown to love her, and she did love me in her own way. Needless to say, there was something missing in our relationship. There was no doubt that Sana had serious psychological problems.

I truly believed that Sana was engaged 15 times because Sana was considered to be one of the most beautiful women in Baghdad. She was well known for her charm and beauty. Wafa, her aunt, told me that she was walking with her father on the street in Baghdad and there was a British man who came up and asked if she could play in one of his movies in London. Of course, Sana's father said "no." He was extremely overprotective of her. Moreover, normally any man who had seen her and asked for her hand found that their relationship did not last longer than one month or so.

Then Sana looked at me with such a mean look and said, "Talib, if you leave like the other men did, I will end your life."

I laughed and said, "You're crazy. I would not leave you. You are the love of my life." She felt good about that and hugged me and kissed me passionately.

It was the last day of the year 2000, and I came home and found Sana preparing a wonderful dinner for us with candlelight, champagne, and delicious food. She was dressed up like a queen, and she said, "Let's you and I celebrate the New Year and get away from the whole world."

I said, "I love you, Baby."

The night of the New Year was young, and we started foreplay. Then, she said, "Stop," and went to the closet and brought out her father's underwear and some of his T-shirts. She put them on her face and started to smell them, and then she said, "Now you can make love to me." I did, while she smelled her father's clothes.

The closer she came to reaching her orgasm, the more she became active in smelling the clothes. And then she said, "Now you need to speak the name of my father and tell me 'you are the daughter of Khalid.'" Of course, that was not his real name. Once I mentioned the name, she reached a really incredible orgasm. She made it easy for me. Once I mentioned her father's name in lovemaking, she had multiple orgasms.

That night was an eye-opening experience with my fiancé, Sana. And, as a psychologist, I could see there was a lot of pathology in our relationship.

One day Sana was out of the house, and I was looking for her, when I received a phone call. She said, "Come and get me. I am on the east side of Detroit."

I asked what had happened to the car, and she said, "I do not know."

I drove all the way to that part of Detroit and found her sitting in her car, oblivious and confused. I talked to her, but she did not talk back to me, she just looked at my face. I said, "Let us go. You can drive your car."

She said, "No. I do not have the key for the car."

I asked, "Where is the key?"

She replied, "I threw it away in the sewage system."

"Why?"

She said, "I do not know. Do not ask me."

So I had to call up my friend to come and open the car door, and then she drove the car back home. When she reached home, she was angry at me, and I did not understand her anger. But I did not make an issue out of it and tried to make excuses for her behavior. She just came to this country, and this was a period of adjustment for her. That is what I told myself, and to just be compassionate with this woman who had lost her father, her country, and her fiancé in Syria. She was going through so many losses.

We were in the sixth month of the relationship, and it seemed like our relationship was in turmoil. I was frustrated with her nonsense and crazy behaviors, but she fulfilled something inside of me. She was a very intelligent woman, and I very much enjoyed the intellectual discussions with her. She had an incredible knowledge about the world, and she was very articulate. Needless to say, she was a showpiece and everyone who saw her just loved her. She had great charm, and she was well-received in any place that we went. She also was very generous in her feelings for me, but seemed to be crazy in her actions to me.

During one of those nights I woke up from such a bad dream. I saw myself drowning in the sea, and then an American submarine came and rescued me. I did not make anything out of it, and I thought it was just gibberish. But, normally, my dreams are accurate.

The next day Wafa, my fiancé's aunt, called up and said she would like to meet with me over a cup of coffee. "But," she said, "Do not tell Sana that you are meeting with me."

I met with Wafa, and she told that a couple days earlier she went over to my home unannounced to see Sana. She found Sana very busy in our bedroom, and she asked Wafa not to come to the bedroom. Sana came out of the bedroom sweating and taking deep breaths. When Wafa had asked her what the matter was, she said, "Nothing." Wafa told me she felt Sana had been up to something evil.

Then Wafa engaged Sana in very light conversation, just to get her mind off the subject. A person from the gas company came to read the meter, and Sana had to go out of the house to meet him. So, Wafa went to the bedroom and found electric wires connected underneath the bed.

Wafa told me, "Sana is planning to electrocute you. And, she had done it before to her last fiancé in Syria."

I said, "What are you saying?"

She said, "Talib, Sana killed the man, and this is the truth, but nobody knows. She connected his body to the electricity and killed him. Our family knows, but we are afraid to say anything. She is also planning to do that to you."

I was baffled.

Wafa explained, "Please, you are my friend, and my niece is crazy, and she wants to end your life before you leave her." She continued, "Please, do not tell her at all."

I said, "Of course," and took a deep breath. "Let me find out for myself," because Wafa tends to feel jealous of Sana.

So, I called up Sana and told her, "I am going to Chicago for a business meeting and I was just informed that I have to go."

I knew she did not like to sleep by herself in the house, and she said she would sleep over at Kathy's home. Kathy was a close friend of ours. I took a room in a local hotel and went at night to my home to see what Wafa had just described to me. Yes, to my astonishment, I found the wires connected to my steel bed.

Let me backtrack for a moment. Before I met Sana, I was dating a woman by the name of Jo, a Voodoo priest. She was one of the finest woman any man could ever have. Jo called me on the phone and said that my life was in danger.

I asked, "How?"

She said that she was reading some spiritual materials and found out that there was a person out there who wanted to hurt me, and she said, "Tee (which is what she normally called me), I love you. Do not lose your life over pussy."

Now, there were three indicators that this woman was up to something evil: my dream, her aunt's story, and my friend Jo's phone call. Thus, I had to treat the matter delicately as to not upset Sana, and to get out of the relationship.

I went home, and acted calmly, and started to sleep on the couch. She wondered why, and I said, "I do not want to sleep with you."

Then I created a fight and told her she would have to leave me for a few days and stay with her aunt. She left home, and then I changed the lock on the door. I told her it was over, without telling her about her intention to kill me.

Normally, I take my vacation in the summertime. The year of 2008, I flew from Abu Dhabi to Detroit, and had to say hello to my friend Kathy. To my surprise, when I went to her house, I found Sana's mother and sister there. They told me that Sana got married after I left her, got divorced, and was now re-married. I was Man Number 16 in her life, and now she was with Man Number 18. Her sister and mother said they still believed that

I was the best man for her. Of course, I said, "Thank you," but I did not mention anything about our relationship.

Conclusion:

There are a several lessons that need to be drawn from this real story.

One, Sana had psychological incest with her father. He did not touch her physically, but he was involved with her psychologically, and that can be as harmful as physical incest. Sometimes, fathers go overboard with their daughters. Sana's father had inflicted serious damage on his daughter, whether or not he was aware of it. A father can be fascinated with his daughter and treat her as if she was his wife. That is what happened to Sana; she was playing the role of the mother, and she was hostile towards her mother because her mother did not protect her. It can happen in a dysfunctional family, and Sana's family was loaded with serious pathology. Thus, the damage was unbearable for her. Because a daughter, in most instances, tends to admire her father's image, she wants to have a man who is similar to her father. Our beloved father, Freud, indicates that women want to marry the image of their father, while a man wants to marry the image of his mother.

Second, we as people tend to be attracted to people who communicate with materials deep in our unconscious mind. For example, I tend to be attracted to sick women because I am a psychologist, and my job is to take care of people. Thus, I have a strong need to heal these women.

Third, some people may want to play the role of being a victim. A relationship is not made in Heaven; it is made in the unconscious mind.

Fourth, we sometimes seek some excitement through turmoil because life can be very boring.

Fifth, we oftentimes feel that all we deserve are people with troubles because we do not value ourselves. This is a self-worth issue.

Sixth, most of men are visual, and beauty can captivate them. They do not look deep into the soul of a person; throughout history man has lost their soul for beautiful woman. Perhaps, we are shallow people.

And, seventh, a dream can be a good indicator of something that may happen in a person's life. Thus, we should not dismiss it.

Box of Identity

A few months ago, I was attending a book review with a group of people. The whole concept of the review was about developing an identity. The question was "Why do people have to have an identity?"

Let us define what we mean by an identity. It is a process by which an individual acquires a sense of being different than another, or it is a set of behaviors or personal characteristics by which an individual is recognized as a member of a group. As a result, an individual so often develops a sense of importance. And when one has a sense of importance, it inevitably creates a division or conflict and it starts first within the self, and second, with others.

Thus, as human beings, we are in constant conflict in having an identity based on, for example, religion, and nationality, color of skin, social class, or geographical location. When we have such an identity, we often want to isolate ourselves from others or scare others so they too will seek their identity. This forces each individual to belong to a certain group, or religion, or race. It seems that the human being who does such is thoughtless because there is nothing one can gain from such an identity, other than pain and suffering.

Human history is replete with a myriad of tragedies because of separation. Now, the inescapable question is this: "Why do we identify?" Perhaps, we have not developed centeredness inside ourselves. There is no inner belonging. Thus, we have to seek outer belonging to give us temporary comfort. Every culture in the world and throughout history has encouraged individuals to identify with certain things. Therefore, we are in a persistent struggle to separate ourselves from others through a box of identity. Consequently, divisions develop such as the separation that threatens certain community groups. Some will arm themselves in order to defend themselves from real or imagined threats. Undoubtedly, most threats are figments of our imagination.

The history of the human community is not a romantic one. It has been and still is colored by wars, pain, and even massacres. Because we are afraid of certain people, we have to attack them and sometime eliminate them. Most of us are guilty of perpetuating such attitudes or beliefs. Sadly enough, our social structure or educational system encourages identification. This leads to separation, separation to fears, and fears to attack. We have to eliminate the sources of fear.

Perhaps, even though we may have a higher degree of knowledge or have an abundance of material possessions, we are insecure because we like to identify with what we have. We separate ourselves from others, and that, in and of itself, create a threat which translates into attack. We see no value in education if it does not free us from the identity box. The concept of identity is not limited to one culture. It seems that almost all cultures have some sort of identification. This is why we see societies as fragmented and in constant competition, rather than cooperating with each other.

The identity box may have different colors and shapes. Some are small, while others are large. But, they are boxes in which the majority of us sit. There is a song by Pete Seeger, an American folk singer, about "Little Boxes". It is about opposition to conformity, where everyone lives in little boxes which all look the same. And also the song is about most educational systems which attempt to conform everyone as well. The song raises the issue of challenging convention and conformity. Although the solution to our box dilemma is a very complicated one and simple at the same time. Basically, we have to free ourselves from the sense of belonging and to challenge conformity.

We just need a different fresh perspective about our existence. We are born in a particular place, at a particular time, and under a particular circumstance. In other words, we are thrown onto the ground of existence (a time, a place, a circumstance) over which we had no choice. This is the existential view. Thus, we need to be more thoughtful about getting out of the box because sitting in a box can deprive us of knowing the real world and force us into becoming a victim of circumstances of our own making that can cause a lot of pain and anguish. We also must not blame others for our pain, but assume the responsibility for it, even though the feeling of being a victim can be very alluring to the human psyche. Nowadays, we see the media celebrating the victim, instead of asking people to take the responsibility of getting out of the box.

Furthermore, the emotionally intelligent individual does not identify with anything, but focuses only on being a human on this planet with the capacity to negotiate conflict because the whole universe is his/her center. We must step out of the box of identity; reach out to other fellow humans, and eliminating separation.

Unfortunately, we consider such a thought a lofty one and difficult to reach. The truth is that every thought or idea started in our head then translates into action. But if it was given to us by another person then that can be second hand thought, because we did not have our own original thought. Then we can discard it and shatter the box, allowing us to breathe the freshness of being free without identification. Identification and separation is quite common among people and it can contribute to the mass pathology in our societies. As Nietzsche so elegantly put it, "Insanity in individuals is something rare, but in groups, parties, nations, and epochs, it is the rule."

THE PROSTITUTE OF HONG KONG

It was 1993 and I was on my way to China to explore the culture and the people, traveling for two weeks to different cities. It is an old culture, and any old culture has many sets of rigid practices. It is the most materialistic culture in the world. People are busy trying to make money, and no one has time to do anything else in life. The life of the Chinese people is cutthroat. There are over one billion people and all of them are competing with each other just to survive. The natural resources are somewhat limited and, therefore, people are always trying to find an alternative to bring a piece of bread to the table. They have no time to acquaint themselves with anything else besides making money. It is a very complicated culture because their souls have been washed in the machine of materialism.

Personally, I did not enjoy China and do not wish to visit again. There are certain countries that have positive energy and amazing attractions, and this energy tends to bring people back again and again or even the desire to settle in those countries. Countries that have positive energy, to mention a few, are: Brazil, Cuba, the Dominican Republic, United Arab Emirates, Morocco, and my beloved country, the United State of America. And, there are certain countries that have negative energy and, once you see them, you do not wish to see them again; for example, Syria, Vietnam, Mali, Iraq, Lebanon, Burma, and China.

The purpose of my trip to China was to learn about the culture and the old method of treatment for various illnesses called acupuncture therapy. It can be a marvelous way of treating illness through less invasive approaches. No doubt, there are a lot of wonderful cultural practices in China which can be appreciated. However, the tone of materialism can be very pronounced in their daily live. Then after the visit to mainland China, I flew back to Hong Kong.

I arrived in Hong Kong in the evening and went to my hotel. In the hotel lobby, I noticed a very attractive Chinese woman sitting and looking at me because I looked like a stranger, and she was in the business of picking up strangers. She was working in the oldest business in the world, prostitution. I took a seat next to her and started up a conversation. We talked about Hong Kong and different topics just to warm up the conversation. Then I asked her to spend the night with me, and she said that would be fine. Normally, I do not treat a prostitute as a prostitute. I treat them as if they were a romantic date. In this way, I can give myself the false feeling of being with my girlfriend and, secondly, I might give the prostitute the feeling that she is a special person--which I really mean. It is a win/win situation.

So, I said, "Susan, how about we go for a dinner in downtown Hong Kong?" She liked the idea very much; right away, I held her hand and pretended she was the love of my life. She liked it very much. I called her "Honey," and she laughed and thought that was very funny.

We had our dinner with candlelight, and I gave her all sorts of compliments. Needless to say, a prostitute needs more compliments than other women because their business is a very hard and difficult one. They have to deal with all kinds of men, and each one needs to be treated differently on the bed.

We finished our dinner at midnight and then took a taxi to my hotel. I held her and was tender with her. Then, I said, "Susan, the night is ours. Please, tell me about the most pleasant experiences in your life, and the most painful one in your life. And, I will do the same."

She really liked the idea. She said, "Talib, there are no pleasant experiences in my kind of life."

I replied, "That is really sad."

"However, my life is filled with painful experiences," and I asked her to please tell me about them. She explained that merely coming to Hong Kong from mainland China is the most horrible experiences any one can face.

Then she looked at me and said, "Talib, you are paying me to have a good time. Why do you want me to bore you with my troubles in life?"

I said, "Susan, you are a worthwhile person, and I love to listen to your story."

"No, I am just a dirty prostitute."

I explained, "No, you are a wonderful human being; it just happens to be that your job is giving pleasure to others, and there's nothing wrong with it."

And, Susan said, "Now you may listen to my whole story."

I am presently 30 years of age and grew up on a very poor peasant farm in the mainland of China. I am the only daughter of my parents. My parents worked and lived on their farm for all their life. We survived all these years with very meager products like rice and soy beans. Then three years ago something very drastic happened to all of the people in my area, and our livelihood has been destroyed.

There was a big company that wanted to build a toy factory in our area. So, they came and confiscated all our land along with that of the rest of the people in the area. The bulldozers came and started to destroy all our agricultural products as well as our houses, and left us helplessly watching our livelihood being taken away. We protested to the central government, but to no avail. We asked the government to give us some compensation; they refused. So, all of the people in the area were homeless with no income. Each of the people in the area tried to set up a tent to protect themselves from the rain and from the cold winter. We wrote letters to the local communist party, but no one was really interested or listened to our plights. Some of the people left the area to live with their relatives in the other parts of China. As far as my parents were concerned, we had no relatives anywhere in China, so we started to live off the handouts from the neighbors.

Then, my father got very sick, and we did not have money for medicine. I was helplessly watching him, emaciated, and my mother who had a serious back problem from the hard labors on the farm for many years. Then, a strange idea came to my mind: I must leave mainland China and go to Hong Kong and find any job to help my family. However, reaching Hong Kong was almost impossible. I had heard that some people swim the sea; some survived, but others died on the way or were caught by the coast guard and sent back to mainland China. However, the idea appealed to me very much, and I thought if I died, I would be happy to be finished with my life of constant struggles. And, if I reached Hong Kong, I would work and send money to my ill parents.

So, I started to ask people about such a journey to Hong Kong. There was a man who knew about such attempts, and he started to advise me on how to manage the perilous journey. He suggested that I get a tube which was used in car tires, a rope to tie the tube around me, a plastic bag with some sweets to eat to give me energy to swim 32 kilometers, and a bottle of water. I prepared everything. He explained that if the coast guard found me, they would send me back to China again, so I had to swim at night and not in daylight. It seemed this man coached people for such journey.

"It may take you four to five days, or even a week, but you have to have very strong tolerance and determination. You also need to know that the sea is filled with sharks; it is up to your luck. If you are lucky, then you will reach Hong Kong. And, if you are not lucky, either the shark will eat you, or you may drown, or the coast guard may bring you back to the mainland. There are a lot of attempts daily by many people who want to escape the mainland and go to Hong Kong. Some of them succeed, and some of them did not."

In spite of all that I had heard, I said to myself, "I will go by any means." There was nothing left for me on the mainland of China, just the suffering and humiliation. I had to sacrifice for my parents. I talked with my parents, but I did not tell them about the dangerous journey. I said I was going by a boat, and they said, "Please, we love you and just take good care of yourself."

I prepared myself mentally for the most dangerous trip across the sea. I kissed my parents goodbye and left from the closet point of the mainland to Hong Kong. I arrived at night and threw myself into the sea with and the tube around my waist. There was tremendous fear inside of me, and my whole body was shivering. I spent the first night in the sea, and the waves were quiet. I was very fearful, lonely, and scared in case I did not make it.

While Susan was telling me her story, I was shaking inside because of what I was hearing. However, I listened to her story without interruption. I was fully with her and following her story verbatim. She continued with her story of the journey in the sea, and she described the second night which was easier than the first. She said there was a feeling of resignation, and that life was worthless; she would either survive or die, it did not matter.

However, there was an upsurge in the feeling of determination that I would make it. Then, I started to focus on how I could reach the shore of Hong Kong. Once in a while, I took a sip of water. During the day, I stayed calm, and during the night I would swim. I ate the few pieces of sweet that I brought with me so I would have some energy. Sometimes, I took a very short nap. By the end of the fourth day, there was nothing left with me, neither water nor food. I was extremely tired, exhausted, and weak, and I looked desperately at the endless sea and the blue sky over me. The thought of death was imminent, and it seemed I was unable to make it.

Then, I remembered my father's illness and the trouble with my family. I looked up to the blue sky and said, "God, can you see me? I need your help. You have created us and now you look at us with disappointment at what we are doing to each other. God, your intention when you created the universe was to have a happy people who loved and helped each other. God, can you hear me? What have I done to deserve such tortures? I am a simple human being who wants to eat a piece of bread with my family. God, I am a victim of human greed and exploitation. God, I am a helpless person who just depends on the mercy of the waves of the sea." Then, in the middle of this dialogue with God, my eyes closed by themselves, and I went into a deep trance.

Something touched my feet, and I was paralyzed by the fear that maybe a shark had come close to me. I was feeling very weak, just barely hanging onto the tube. This was my fourth day in the sea. I kept quiet, with no movement. The fifth night came. I was pushing myself so slowly with no energy left in me. Then, lo and behold, I heard some voices which meant that I was close to the shore of Hong Kong.

Now, there was a glimmer of hope; I could see the light of Hong Kong, and there was a boat of fisherman. They saw me, and they came to me. They wanted to pick me up, but I said "No." I was fearful of them. They talked to me in my native language and told me they would help me out and not to worry. They said, "Congratulations. Now you are in Hong Kong."

I went with them with the last breath of my life. One of them took me to his small home, and his wife fed me some fish and rice. I slept for two days, and then I was able to move around, but my body was still very weak. I stayed with them for one month. Then, the wife of the fisherman put me up with a rich Chinese family, working for them illegally to clean their house. However, that family was very abusive, and they beat me up if they found a speck of dust in the house. I endured much abuse from this family for one year because I had to be patient so I could get some money to send to my parents.

One day, I was going to buy some fruits and vegetables for the family at the local market. A Chinese man came to me and said, "You have a very gorgeous body, and you look attractive. "Why don't you work as a prostitute? You will make a lot of money. Just try it, and if you do not like it, you can always leave."

The man approached me during the lowest point of my life. I got into the business, and I have been doing it for two years.

Susan finished telling me her story, and I was very sad about her. Inside of me the story stirred up strong emotion about human conditions. At that minute, I felt the triumph of the human spirit over all the obstacles that she had faced. A peasant woman did a remarkable job just to make a difference in the lives of the people around her. I held her in my arms and said, "Susan, you are such a great woman. I am really very happy I met you." We did not sleep that night and neither did we make love. The story was so overwhelming.

The next day she stayed with me, and we went sightseeing together in Hong Kong. Then, at night we went for dinner, and when we were back at the hotel, she said, "Talib, I do not feel good about myself, selling my body."

I said, "You do not sell your body; you actually rent one part of your body. You are like any one of us, normally. We rent a part of our body. For example, the solider rents his hands to the army. If he had no hands, he would not be a soldier. The carpenter rents his hands, as well, to make a table or a chair for us. I am a psychologist; I rent my tongue or my language to treat people, and if I was a mute person, then I would not be able to be a psychologist, and so on.

She said, "If every one of us is renting a part of their body, then I am renting my vagina for a short period of time."

I said, "Yes!"

She said, "How about the woman who rents her womb for carrying a pregnancy for others? Is she like me as well?"

I said, "No doubt."

"So," she said, "why do we place so much value on the vagina, and why is this part of our body more valuable than the rest of our body parts?"

I said, "Susan, throughout the history of humanity, we have placed too much value on the vagina because of our selfish nature. We want the woman just for us alone but we also appreciate virginity for the same reason." I continued, 'This subject has been dealt with by Herman Hass, the German writer who talked about it in his book *Golden Bond and Neurosis*. Susan, this is a very difficult and sensitive concept, and people may find it hard to digest."

She said, "Even women do not like me."

And I said, "Perhaps, they are jealous of you because you make more money then they do."

I said, "Susan, do not pay attention to what people may say. Try to follow your own direction. Do you like what you do?" And she replied that she did not. "Then what do you like to do?"

She said, "My dream is to marry a man from the west and have children with him and help my family."

I asked, "Why from the west?"

"I do not like Chinese men."

"Why?"

"They are very greedy and boring people." Then, she continued, "Talib, since I came to Hong Kong, I have learned many things about mainland China."

"What did you learn?"

"China is the most polluted place in the world. China is not a happy place by any measure. Chinese people can sell contaminated baby milk to the world, or toys that have lead in them and children get poisoned. They are not conscientious people. Their unbridled greed controls them."

I explained that they were no different from other people, and she said, "No, they are different."

"In what way?" I asked.

"Normally western individuals have some mercy in their hearts, but the Chinese have no compassion in their hearts."

I said, "Susan, now I rest my case. I do not like to pass judgment on people."

"What is wrong with passing judgment on people?" she asked. "Even, God who created us judges us."

I explained that I had learned to accept people the way they were. She said that was a lofty concept. "You will never accept people the way they are. We pass judgment all the time, either on things or people."

She continued, "Talib, the reality of the matter is that we live in a world of people. There are good people, and there are evil people and there are nasty ones and there are benevolent people. Thus, passing judgment is imperative. Look at my situation. People pass judgment on me, and they call me a prostitute, a word that carries a bad connotation, instead of calling me an entertainer. I sell a pleasure to make a man happy so he can be productive and less mean to his family and others. If the sexual drive builds up inside a man, he can be very aggressive to others. I am providing a very essential service to mankind."

PREVIOUS LIFE

Haroon was a 46-year-old male who came to see me for treatment of his addiction to alcohol while I was working in Abu Dhabi. Normally, I use a psychoanalytical approach to deal with addiction. That approach requires deeply delving into the past to find out about the roots of pathology in the life of the addict. Haroon was working for the police force, and he played the lute and sang. People liked to drink with him because he entertained them. He had twin daughters, and he had recently been divorced because of his drinking problem. He lived by himself and felt very lonely. Then, in one of our therapeutic sessions, he told me the following amazing story.

✤　✤　✤

I grew up in Dubai, and I am the only son of my parents. While I was a teenager, I used to have a constant dream about one particular woman who I would always see myself walking with on the beach of Dubai. The dream has been with me from age 16 to age 18, almost for two years. At that time, I did not understand why such a dream came to me. I informed my parents about it, and they said a teenager always dreams of women because that is the peak of their sexual arousal.

I became very keen in describing the woman in detail. I even drew her picture. I would describe her as a rather medium-sized woman with brown skin, dark jet black hair and dark black eyes, with large bosom, and a very curvy sexy body. The dream was a happy one. She would just come and talk

to me, I would hold her hand, and we would walk on the beach of Dubai.
I do not remember the core of the conversation with her. I asked myself
several times why such a specific woman came to me for a long time. I have
no answer. She even told me her name in the dream was Nora.

Then after the age 18, I joined the UAE Army and became a solider
for four years, and then I left the Army and joined the police force. In
the meantime, the dream stopped, and I felt really sad, and would like to
have had the dream back. She had just become like my companion in the
dream.

At age 26 years, one of my colleagues in the police force by the name of
Adam asked me, "Why aren't you married yet?"

I said, "As you know, marriage can cost a lot of money in the UAE,
and I came from a very poor family, and I do not have money to have a wife
from the UAE."

Then my friend told me that there were a lot people who felt the same.
And, everyone knew that if you had a wife from the UAE that could cost
you an arm and a leg. He said that was why some people from the UAE went
to Yemen and India to get a wife because it was cheaper and did not cost a
lot. So, I asked what the solution might be. Adam said, "Let us go together
to Yemen to find a wife for you and me."

I said, "I like the idea very much," and we both arranged for the trip. We
took a one-month vacation, and we flew to Sanaa, the capital of Yemen.

We arrived there and in the morning we went wandering in the streets
of Sanaa. We did not know anybody, or how to start to look for a wife. Then,
we took a taxi to go to see the old part of the town, just for sightseeing. We
engaged in a small conversation with the taxi driver, and he asked us where
we were from. We told him we were from the UAE, and then he asked us
why we had come to Yemen. We told him that we came to Yemen to look
for brides. He looked at us, and he said he would help us if we were sincere.
And, we said, "We really are strangers, and we do not know anyone in
Yemen, and we would appreciate any help from you."

He was a very friendly man, and he suggested the following. He said,
"Listen, folks, Sanaa is in the northern part of Yemen, and people here
tend to be very conservative. They do not give their women to an outsider.
The best place for you to find a wife is the southern part of Yemen which is

Aden. The people in the south are friendly and welcome the outsider. Then, he said, "I will be more than happy to take you to the south and introduce you to the people down there. We may find brides for both of you."

So, we went back to the hotel, took our luggage, and he drove us to the southern part of Yemen. It took us almost one day to drive. We arrived at night, and he found us a room in a cheap hotel because neither of us had a lot of money--just enough for the trip. We slept that night with the taxi driver, all in one room. In the morning we had our breakfast, and then he took us to one of his old friends and introduced us to him. He asked his friend to help us to find brides.

The friend was happy to do that, because in the Islamic religion, it is considered a virtue and a great deed if you help someone to get married. The friend of the taxi driver said, "Let us start with Haroon, and then we will help Adam."

He made a few phone calls, and he said, "There is a family who are very good people. They have one daughter who lives with her mother, and her father is deceased. She is about 26 years old. She has half-brother who does not live with them. We can go and visit them."

I said, "Fine. It is close to my age," and we all drove to the home where her half-brother greeted us at the door.

In the Arab culture, when a man comes to ask for the hand of a woman, she comes and brings the tea to him and to the rest of the guests. She sits with him for a short period of time, and then she leaves. Then the guest asks, "Shall we drink the tea?" and if they say, "Drink the tea," it is the sign of approval to the man.

So, the door opened, and the woman entered the room holding the tea tray, and she greeted us. I took one look at her, and I literary freaked out. I started to cry, laugh, scream, and acting like insane man saying, "She is the one in my dream; this is Nora."

She dropped the tray and went running to her mother, crying and screaming as well, and saying, "He is the one in my dream."

The people in the room were her half-brother, my friend Adam, the taxi driver, and his friend from Aden. None of them understood what had happened, and all of them were bewildered and shocked. The others started to hold me and calm me down, but my body was shaking, and then I went into a deep trance, leaving the real world for a minute or so. They asked me, "What is going on with you, Haroon?"

I said, "I saw her in my dreams for two years a long time ago. She is going to be my wife."

They thought I was out of my mind. They even thought there may have been some black magic done on me. Her half-brother looked at the man that brought us to him and said, "Why did you bring me crazy people?"

I woke up and said, "Please, listen to my story," and I told them that for over two years I had seen this woman come to me in my dreams, and her name was Nora. Here, everyone started to recite some versus from the Quran, and there was an atmosphere of silence and anticipation in the room.

Then, her half-brother brought Nora [that is her real name which 1 know it before 1 saw her] and her mother to the guest room, and when we were all in one room, he said to Nora, "Tell us the story."

She said that once she entered the room and saw Haroon, she could not control herself because she had seen him in her dreams, and his name was Haroon. She pointed at me several times and said with such nervousness, "Tell me your name. Is it Haroon?"

I said, "Yes."

She said, "You will be my husband," and then she asked, "Are you like my father, playing music?"

I said, "Yes."

She asked, "Do you lie or do you tell the truth?"

I said, "No, this is the truth."

And then she jumped from her seat, went inside the home, and brought the lute. She said, "This is my father's lute. I kept it all these years for you because you told me in the dream that you play music. You can play it if you are really Haroon."

I picked up the lute and started to play wonderful music for them and sing very sad songs about life and how much we are unfortunate people to live in a world of deceit, lies, and abuses. Everyone in the room started to cry. Then, I put the lute down, and we all felt that something unusual had happened to all of us. We all looked down at the ground, and we were speechless for a while. Language was not enough to describe what had transpired at that moment.

However, the mother had kept silent all this time; then she spoke. "Listen, folks. That is very true. My daughter used to come to me very often and tell me that she saw in her dream a man by the name of Haroon and how similar to her father he is. He is a musician like her father. I always thought that my daughter, Nora, may have been hallucinating because of the loss of her father, but now, it seems, everything has come full circle.

It seemed an extraordinary story. They agreed that the wedding should take place right away. Nora and Haroon got together, and it seemed they just belonged to each other.

Nora's half-brother arranged for a big wedding party and announced it all over Aden. They invited all the musicians in town. Because her father had been a well-known and highly respected musician, the musicians in Aden wanted to celebrate his daughter's wedding and pay attribute to him. It was a big party, the music lasted all night long, and everyone had a great time. It was like putting closure on her father's death with this celebration. The marriage was consummated, and Nora and Haroon became husband and wife.

During an evening time, Nora and I were walking on the beach of Aden. Nora took a pondering look at me and said, "You are my husband, and you need to know about the most important thing that happened in my life."

I said, "Sure, please tell me."

She said, "It is about my father. He did not die; he was killed."

I asked how he was killed, and she said, painfully, "My mother killed him," and then she started to cry. She told me to listen to the whole story:

Nora said, "My father was a very handsome man and an accomplished musician in Yemen. There were a lot of women who were interested in seeing him, and he was a womanizer. He used to go out with different women, and, as you know, Haroon, this is the life of a musician. My mother felt very jealous of that and decided to teach him a lesson. She boiled very hot water and while he was sleeping, she took the water and poured it over his penis. They took him to the hospital, but he had lost his penis. It was melted because of the extremely hot water. And after 10 days, he died in the hospital. The police brought my mother to the Court, and they convicted her to 10 years in the prison. However, before my father's death, he pardoned her and asked to release her. On his deathbed, he forgave her and said; 'There is no point to have her in the prison. Let her be out to raise up my beautiful daughter, Nora.' He was truly a noble man. In spite of his forgiveness, my mother spent three years in the prison. I was 14 years old at the time of the incident, and now I am 26 years old. Twelve years have passed, but still the painful memory of my father is carved in my mind."

"I have lived all my life struggling with the fact that my mother murdered my father, and she took him away from me. She deprived me of his love and care. Sometimes I am outraged at her, and other times, I pity her. Also, she did not get married after his death. As you can see, she is a very pretty woman and there were a lot of men interested in marrying her, but she refused. She dedicated her life to raising me up. She has also lived with a lot of pain. She is an out-cast by the family of my father, and even now some neighbors call her a killer. As you can see, Haroon, our life was not a happy one, and now you stepped in to marry me. I may ask God to grant me the strength, the patience, and the compassion to clear up my heart from any hurt and be your supportive wife, and make you the happiest man in the world. I was dreaming of you and, finally, God brought you to me from a far distance. I am deeply thankful to the positive power in the world. That was the best reward for me after the loss of my father."

Then I spoke and said, "Nora, I will try to do my best to make you happy. You are my soul mate, and you have been in my dreams for a good period of time. Perhaps God has brought our spirits together so we can have a wonderful family."

I went back to the UAE to arrange for my bride to come and, after a couple of weeks, she came. My aging parents received her with such love and embraced her with kindness. We lived a very enjoyable life together. Nora gave me twin girls, and she showered me with such love and respect. She was the best wife any man could have.

Then, 10 years ago, I was introduced to alcohol, and now I cannot help myself. The alcohol took complete control of me. I have been involved in many traffic accidents, and I was jailed several times. I started not going to my work, and they have given me several warnings. I lost a lot of money and deprived my family of many things just to supply my addiction. I felt down on myself.

As a result of the alcohol abuse, I developed another health problem and I began to sweat excessively. Summer or winter, I had to change my garments several times a day, and no one knew the medical reason for this. As a result of sweating, life for me became unbearable. I even sweat in my sleep. I woke up at night and felt as if I was swimming in a pool of water.

The other part of the addiction is that I became a very angry man, and I used my hand a few times with my wife. Thus, she left me, took the girls and filed for divorce. I became a very lonely man, but also very serious about stopping the addiction and restoring myself and my family.

✢   ✢   ✢

I have worked with Haroon and have included his ex-wife in our therapeutic sessions; she was receptive to helping him out. He has stopped his addiction. She let him come home to stay with the girls because she started to work. During that time, her mother died. As far as Haroon's excessive sweating is concerned, the police department was planning to send him to Germany for a treatment in which they may cut out his sweat glands.

I have concluded my therapy with him because he stayed sober for over eight months without any relapse. A few months after the closure of therapy, I gave him a call, and he told me he was "off and on" with his wife. He did inform me of the amazing and rewarding fact that both of his daughters are involved in music, and they have excelled in playing the lute and the piano. I said, "The apple does not fall far from the tree."

The merit of this story is that spirits can meet in a different world, in a previous life, you may say. Perhaps, this is not the only life that we have lived. We may have lived many lives before this one. Is there any doubt that Haroon and Nora met before, and they came into contact again in our visible life? There is some evidence supporting that. It is also suggested that there are kindred spirits who have met before or lived together in different forms.

There are two kinds of worlds, the invisible world that we might call the spirit world, and the visible world that we might call the tangible world. Normally, the invisible world is very vast, limitless, beyond our limited comprehension, and beyond the knowledge of our five senses. The invisible world tends to rule or control or even manages the visible world.

We are a spiritual being in a human body. The spirit is eternal, but our body is a collection of temporary experiences. Our body is just like a bag of meat carrying our spirit for the interval period of time between birth and death. Then, the spirit leaves the body and moves to a different realm, while our body disintegrates to its original component which is the clay.

www.ingramcontent.com/pod-product-compliance
Lightning Source LLC
Chambersburg PA
CBHW022249290526
45785CB00015B/446